On Stage & In Shadows

To Nat and Luke ~

Love,

Marie Wallace

On Stage & In Shadows

✦

a career memoir

Marie Wallace

iUniverse, Inc.
New York Lincoln Shanghai

On Stage & In Shadows
a career memoir

Copyright © 2005 by Marie Wallace

iUniverse books may be ordered through booksellers or by contacting:

iUniverse
2021 Pine Lake Road, Suite 100
Lincoln, NE 68512
www.iuniverse.com
1-800-Authors (1-800-288-4677)

ISBN-13: 978-0-595-35877-9 (pbk)
ISBN-13: 978-0-595-80334-7 (ebk)
ISBN-10: 0-595-35877-2 (pbk)
ISBN-10: 0-595-80334-2 (ebk)

Printed in the United States of America

To my dear mother, Dorothy Nellie Maass Wallace, who managed the house and our family expertly and with little or no help. I will be forever grateful to her for the grace and wisdom she possessed, and all the sacrifices she made. Somehow, she always managed to give all her children just what we needed, and to teach us lasting lessons and values. She was my biggest supporter, and she convinced me that I could do anything I set out to do.

Contents

Foreword by Jonathan Frid xi

Preface by Ruth Buzzi xii

Introduction xiv

Beginnings: One More Mouth to Feed 1

Getting Started 9

Sophocles' *Electra & Harlequinade* 17

Gypsy 23

Wedding Bells 35

That's *The Beauty Part* 41

Everybody Loved the *Albatross* 49

Segue into *Angel Street* 55

The Hampton Playhouse 59

The Right Honourable Gentleman: Back To My British Accent 70

Sweet Charity 77

Dark Shadows 85

Somerset: Vampire Lady Joins Upper Middle Class 101

The Women: How Catty Can You Get? 107

Mert & Phil 113

Meadow Brook Theatre 117

Sly Fox: How Sweet It Was!. 125

Carousel. 130

Last Licks. 137

On the Road Again 140

East Meets West 145

Back to New York...or Was I?. 152

The Lion in Winter: Jonathan Frid Takes Me To College. 159

Blowing Rock 165

Photography: A New Beginning 170

Jonathan, Marie, the Lion, and Me: A Note from
    David Moore 177

Career Highlights 181

About the Author by Craig Hamrick 185

Acknowledgements

I would like to offer my wholehearted thanks to my editors Craig Hamrick and Michael Karol for their tremendous help and thoughtful guidance; and to David Moore for encouraging the writing of this book and for his help and suggestions throughout.

The photos and other memorabilia are from my private collection. The Internet Broadway Database (www.ibdb.com), the Lortel Archives for Off-Broadway (www.lortel.org/LLA_archive/index.cfm), and the Internet Movie Database (www.imdb.com) were invaluable in helping me sort out production dates and players. The New York Library of the Performing Arts was a veritable treasure trove of information.

I deeply appreciate contributions from Ruth Buzzi, Jim Pierson, Marcy Robin, and Jonathan Frid. I also want to thank my family for their unending support.

Foreword

Marie Wallace has given us a book spilling over with a wonderful collection of memories of a lifetime, which has taken her through a world rich in associations with the glamorous whirlwind of Broadway and television.

Twice she has tangoed with yours truly in such whereabouts as ABC-TV's *Dark Shadows* studio in New York and, during my first outing as a stage director, at Georgia College in Milledgeville, Georgia. There, Marie played—with great panache and style—Eleanor of Aquitaine in *The Lion in Winter.* She made my job that much easier, and I thank her for sharing some moments of her amazing life with me and, now, with all of you.

Jonathan Frid
Canada
May 2005

Preface

I've always thought that my dear friend Marie Wallace belongs in the White House. She has grace, intelligence, beauty, sincerity, kindness, and an incredible knack for making you feel that you're really special. These traits would make her the perfect First Lady. But since she doesn't have any political aspirations, I consider her the First Lady of Broadway.

Marie and I met when we were cast in the original Broadway production of Bob Fosse's *Sweet Charity* starring Gwen Verdon. During that period, I got to meet her wonderful husband, Dr. Greg Pollock, whom I'll never forget. He had a very warm, genteel manner, with a quiet sense of humor—a fine man indeed. It was wonderful to see how proud he was to have snatched such a prize as Marie. He loved that she was an actress on Broadway and was very supportive in every way. They made a terrific couple.

During the year-and-a-half run of *Charity*, Marie and I had dressing rooms that were right next to each other on the theatre's top floor. Not only did we become great friends because of that proximity, we actually became sewing buddies, too. I had some free time between scenes, and since I was interested in sewing, I asked the seamstresses who made all of our costumes what kind of sewing machine I should get. They recommended a small portable Singer model called the "Featherweight 221." It only sews forward and backward, but that's all I needed it to do. I mentioned it to my parents and they bought me one for my birthday. I brought it right to the theatre to show it off and decided to keep it on my long dressing room counter. Marie's schedule matched mine, so we were off stage at the same time. She brought in her own portable and as we happily stitched away and chatted, we established the foundation of a beautiful friendship. Betsy Ross had nothing on us!

Because everyone in the cast and crew knew we did a lot of sewing, at one point during the run the show's stage manager, Michael Sinclair, asked the two of us to help him make a Noah's Ark gift for Gwen and Bob's daughter, Nicole. Michael built the Ark, and Marie and I burned the candles at both ends making dozens of small, cloth stuffed animals with our sewing machines, and by hand, stopping repeatedly to run down five flights of stairs to perform our parts on the Palace Theatre stage.

Since then, we've managed to keep up with one another even though we live three thousand miles apart. Over the years, we've checked on each other by phone, and these days, we've kept up with the times and are e-mail buddies. We've even linked our Web sites. When we're in New York or Los Angeles at the same time, we always make it a point to get together at a nice restaurant, and no matter how long it's been, we pick up the last conversation we were having as if it was just the day before.

Marie happens to be a very gifted photographer, and she's focused on me several times throughout the years, including once when she created one of my favorite headshots right in front of my California home, and another time when she shot me when I was dolled up as Little Bo Peep for the first of several Macy's Thanksgiving Day Parades I've been in.

The one thing I would love Marie to do for me: make and send me a loaf of her great Wheat Germ Bread, which tastes like dessert, so I can have it with a cup of coffee while I begin to read the stories in this book with lots of love and enthusiasm.

Bring 'em on, Marie.

Ruth Buzzi
Hollywood
May 2005

Introduction

I have been an actress since I was a teenager and, in the early years of my career, I did a great deal of work in the theatre. Interestingly enough, it was only after I began to appear on television's *Dark Shadows* that I had a fan club and the notoriety that comes with being on a popular TV show. Even today, more than thirty years after filming the last show, I can walk down the street, or ride on a bus, or sit in a restaurant or theatre, and someone will recognize me. But the recognition is usually of me as Eve or Megan or Crazy Jenny from *Dark Shadows*. So when author Craig Hamrick was creating a Web site called Dark Shadows Online (www.darkshadowsonline.com) and invited me to be part of it, I thought it was a great idea. Each actor featured on the site had a separate section, and he eventually worked it out so that those sections became individual sites—mine becoming MarieWallace.com.

We decided to do a section called "Marie's Scrapbook" to introduce fans to my very varied theatrical background. I wrote a few stories about stage shows I had appeared in, and found the related photos, and put them on the site. The fan reaction was very enthusiastic, but they wanted to know more. There's a *Dark Shadows* Festival every year, and fans always come loaded down with questions about our past and present work, and no matter how many answers we have, there's always a desire for additional information. I dug around in my theatrical trunk (figuratively speaking—it was actually envelopes and boxes in corners and shelves of many different closets), and I found a lot of interesting material. Photographs, playbills, reviews, and other memorabilia all began to appear. It was great fun to rediscover each item: a picture I hadn't seen in years, a ticket stub, or an article in a newspaper that I'd long forgotten.

I got involved in my story and its progression, and before I knew it, there was enough to fill a book. I decided that, instead of putting scattered stories on my site, I would share the whole tale by reconstructing my theatrical journey on stage and in *Dark Shadows*. I've had a wonderful trip, with so many supportive people around me, and I hope to pass on the enthusiasm and passion I have for my profession through this memoir.

Marie Wallace
New York City
May 2005

Beginnings:
One More Mouth to Feed

I'm a rare bird—a native New Yorker. Not too many who call themselves New Yorkers can say that. I was born in the heart of New York City in a hospital on Roosevelt Island; not in the Bronx, or Brooklyn, or Queens, but in *Manhattan...The Big Apple...home of The Great White Way*. And when I came screaming into this big city, there were already four other kids in the Wallace household—my big brother, Bobby, who was seven years old; a five-year-old sister, Margie; and the twins, Dolly and Billy, who were not yet three years of age. My parents certainly had their hands full, especially my mother, who did the bulk of the household work.

Roosevelt Island is just across the East River from Manhattan, and was reached via the 59th Street Bridge, better known as The Queensboro Bridge. There were two trolley lines on the outer lanes of the lower level of the bridge. The service went back and forth between stations at each end of the bridge, with a stop right above the island. Then, you had to take an elevator down to the street level. The bridge wasn't that far from where my family lived, on the Upper East Side of Manhattan in a section called Yorkville. My father picked us up at the hospital, and we're probably lucky that we got home, since he arrived rather tipsy, or so my mother later told me. He was Irish, so *everything* was cause for celebration. But we did arrive home safely, and I joined the crowded household.

The Yorkville section of Manhattan begins around 65th Street and extends north to 96th Street, stretching east to west from York Avenue to Lexington Avenue. It was also called *Germantown* back then. The name didn't come about because of the ethnic make-up of its residents, but rather due to all the German restaurants, sausage shops, bakeries, and turnvereins (gymnasiums).

We were a very diversified neighborhood, with Irish, Italian, Czechoslovakian, German, Greek, Puerto Rican, and Hungarian immigrants, plus second generations, all living side-by-side. The heart of the area was at 86th Street, between First and Lexington Avenues. It was our amusement area, a mini-Broadway, with three movie houses; clubs that offered dancing and entertainment; Horn & Har-

1

dart's Automat; the best ice-cream parlor in the neighborhood, Bunny's (where they slathered delicious pastel shades of whipped cream on top of the most scrumptious ice-cream sundaes...and the sugar cones were pretty great, too); loads of clothing and shoe stores; and wonderful ethnic restaurants including The Brauhaus and The Ideal. My favorite dish at both German restaurants was Wiener schnitzel (veal fillets, pounded flat, dipped in eggs, covered with bread crumbs, and lightly fried). There was also a bakery, Kleiner Konditorie, and I loved everything it sold—most especially the linzer tart (raspberry jelly inside crispy, butter cookies, topped with sugar). It was considered an outing to go up to 86th, and we always had great fun there.

On Saturdays, I spent the day at the Monroe movie house, closer to home, on First Avenue at 76th Street. (Years later, it became a television studio, where I did one of my first small parts on a TV variety show with Henny Youngman.) There were many winter Saturdays when we entered the theatre at noon, with the sun shining, only to come out five hours later to a dark and snowy evening. These days I can barely sit through a two-hour movie, but back then we saw two features, a cartoon, a newsreel, coming attractions, a horse race (the lights went up after the race, and kids with the winning numbers received gifts), and one chapter from a series like *Batman*, *Spiderman*, or *Superman* (we had no female celluloid superheroes in the fifties).

One of my favorite adventures as a kid was the short trip with my mother to Rockwell's Bakery on 75th Street, where we bought the greatest dessert: lemon-meringue pie. She also always bought whole wheat bread for us, while the other neighborhood kids ate white bread. She listened to Carlton Fredericks, one of the first famous nutritionists with a radio show, and followed most of his advice. (Our desserts were usually fresh fruits, but every once in a while she did allow us to have sinful desserts like lemon-meringue pie.) I didn't realize it then, but early on, Mom got me on the road to healthy eating, which I've stayed on throughout my life.

When we were teenagers, my friends and I went to a club called the Corso for Latin dancing and to meet boys. We also went to the church dances on Sunday nights at St. Josephs, located at 97th Street and Lexington Avenue, and at St. Ignatius, at 84th off Park Avenue. In New York at that time, every block in the city was like a small town; everything you could need or want was available within one square block.

On our block, there were three grocery stores; we went to Moxin's most of the time, but if our bill was running too high and we weren't ready (or able) to pay it, we'd drop by one of the other two. We also had two tailors, three beer gardens, two barbers, one tailor/cleaner, one shoe cobbler, a plumber, the Republican and the Democratic Social Clubs, a laundry, a junk shop, and a wood factory. My favorites were the two candy stores—Joe Zoler's and Mike's—where we ordered egg creams. God knows where that name came from, since there's no egg or cream in them (they're actually made from one cup of milk, one cup of cold seltzer, and four tablespoons of chocolate or vanilla syrup), but they were very popular and sweet, and if we had five cents, we bought one. Candy stores like Zoler's and Mike's don't exist anymore, but it's where we hung out, reading all the magazines on the rack, making our phone calls, and buying our occasional egg cream, until we were thrown out of the tiny shop to make room for better-paying customers.

Burton's ice cream parlor was near York Avenue, with a jukebox in the backroom, where teenagers like my sister Margie and brother Bobby would jitterbug. The younger kids (Dolly, Billy, and I) could only peek in, but as long as we got ice cream cones (our older siblings would buy them for us), we were satisfied. Medicraft's, a nurse's uniform shop, was on the other side of the street, which was very convenient for the nurses at New York Hospital, across York Avenue. When Medicraft expanded, it replaced Burton's, much to our dismay.

The Third Avenue El (elevated train) was there, with trolley cars running below it. (The El and the trolley cars are now gone.) My brothers were more adventurous than we girls were, and they often rode it all the way down to Chinatown. And although it was illegal to sell firecrackers to minors, they always managed to buy them for our July 4th celebration. The Lenox Hill Settlement House (an after-school boy's and girl's club where I learned how to swim) was just up the street and across First Avenue, and the tenements that housed my childhood friends, Margie, Yvonne, Joannie, Dotty, Anne, Helen, and Mary, were all located on 70th Street.

On St. Patrick's Day, there would be an Irish Night in the auditorium of St. Catherine's of Siena, on 69th Street. The kids sold tickets many weeks in advance, and there was always great excitement about who the guest artist would be. Every year there were rumors that Frank Sinatra might appear, and every year, on the night of March 17, the priest would read a telegram from Sinatra with the same message, "Sorry I can't join you, but I'm sending my best friend in my place." And, I don't know how they swung it, but some stars *did* come to this neighborhood church. I think it was because the priests were friends of Nick Kenny and Walter Winchell, important columnists of the day. Some of the stars that visited our neighborhood included Nat King Cole (we heard him sing *Nature Boy* for the first time), Vic Damone (a rising star, he appeared at the Paramount Theater on Broadway weeks later and was an immediate hit), and Jimmy Durante (little did I know, enjoying his work that night, that *I'd* be onstage with him years later).

I attended PS 82, just up the block from our apartment, on the corner of 70th Street and First Avenue. It was an elementary school starting with kindergarten and Mrs. Goldstone, and ending at 6th grade with Mrs. Adler. From there I went to PS 183, a junior high school, on 66th Street between York and First Avenues. That building is still there and remains a school, and in 2003, my sister Dolly and I went to its one hundreth anniversary celebration. Now, on Saturdays, there's a green grocer and flea market in the schoolyard. Every once in a while, when I'm on the East Side on a weekend, I walk around the schoolyard thinking about what I might have been doing that same day all those years ago, or who I was talking to. I was twelve or thirteen years old then, so my friends and I were probably talking about life in general and boys in particular.

When I graduated from 183, I wore a dress I'd made myself, as did all of my schoolmates (it was a class project—we didn't have a choice). At that time, they were still giving courses in cooking and sewing for girls, while the boys took shop, or were involved in sports. My graduation outfit was white rayon, with a very flared skirt, cap sleeves, and a detachable peplum (a short section attached to waistline of a dress), which was the "in" fashion of the day. It was really quite wonderful. All those sewing classes had paid off; I became a good dressmaker and designer. There would even come a time, during my theatrical career, when I'd make my own costume for a Broadway show. But more about that later.

I got into sports too, just not in school. I played such games as Kick the Can, Stoop Ball, Nibs (marbles played on the top of an intricate man-hole cover in the street), King, Ringalevio, and Touch Football. No fancy sports for me.

We played regular football too, but again, we improvised by using a paper football made by folding and rolling up an entire newspaper and wrapping it with string or rubber bands. We also had four-wheeled roller skates that were put on over our shoes, and we had a key to tighten them. When the skates got very old, the more enterprising boys, like my brothers, took them apart and made skateboards or scooters with them. We were doing all this out on the street; the traffic was minimal compared to today, and when a car approached, we'd say, "Hold it," and they'd stop! We'd finish the play, pause, watch the car pass by, and resume play.

From an early age, I've always had a very straightforward, honest approach to things (probably because my mom always taught us to tell the truth), but I had some experiences at school that made me wish I had been more comfortable stretching the truth. In my first high school (Mabel Dean Bacon High), I once played hooky to go to the St. Patrick's Day Parade, along with more than half the class (maybe even half the school). The next day my teacher asked each student why she was absent, which was the usual routine. My friend Joannie and I decided we'd tell the truth, thinking that, at the very least, the teacher would respect our honesty. We knew everyone would lie and say, "I had a sore throat," or "I had a 103-degree fever." What an insult to the teacher's intelligence. That's what *we* thought…. We were wrong!

We proudly stood up and said, "We weren't sick, we went to the parade." Our teacher reprimanded us and marched us down to the principal's office with a pink slip, a punishment worse than death. It meant that one of your parents had to come in and talk to the principal. Well, that did it. I told my mother I didn't like the policies of that school and that I wanted to transfer to another one. She supported me, as she always did, and Joannie and I transferred from there to Julia Richman High.

This school was much more convenient for me since it was at 67th Street, just a stone's throw from our apartment. I originally chose the other school just to be different from my friends, but it was a long bus ride away. Saving all that time on travel really worked better for me, because it gave me lots of time to get involved with my "play acting."

My love of acting took root in my church, Christ Church Methodist, at 60th Street and Park Avenue, which was about a fifteen-block walk from our house. My mother insisted that we attend Sunday school every week and she picked the best place to go. Christ Church had the most wonderful minister, a man named Ralph W. Sockman, who was well-known through his radio program, *The National Radio Pulpit,* and a nationally syndicated newspaper column, *A Lift for Living.* He became a role model for me—not that I wanted to be a minister, but something about his personality and his teachings really hit home for me. He was the most elegant man I had ever seen, and he had a glorious voice. If he had chosen to be a Shakespearean actor, he would have been the greatest we've ever heard. And, just as important, that's where the theatrical bug really bit me. At first I was just reading the Bible aloud in class, and the teacher complimented me on my voice. From that point on, I worked to make it as mellifluous as possible, at least to my own ears.

One day I discovered that the church had a stage and auditorium in its basement, and a group called the Park Avenue Players. I joined the company immediately and found that many professional actors and directors would work there when they were between paid engagements. (I use the term *work* but, of course, no one ever was paid for that work.) Even our set designer, Bill Pitkin, later became a Broadway designer (1954's *Threepenny Opera*, 1967's *The Impossible Years*, and 1973's *42 Seconds from Broadway*, just to name a few). We worked together professionally after that, in my second Broadway show, *The Beauty Part*. Our star was a real beauty in that show, but we'll get to that in a later chapter. I was in good company at the Park Avenue Players with all those pros around, and the group proved to be a good training ground for me.

My first audition ever was for the Players' production of *I Remember Mama*. I was the youngest girl at the audition, so you'd think I'd get cast as one of the many ingénues in the play. However, I was also the tallest, so they asked me to read for the older characters. Mama was already cast, with a really old woman of about twenty-five, or at least she seemed old to me since I was about thirteen. I ended up playing "Aunt Jenny," Mama's sister. (I played an ingénue once; in my first professional stage appearance: Terrence Rattigan's *Harlequinade*, but that was it! After that, it was always the femme fatale, the other woman, the villain, the hooker, the rich bitch—all the fun parts.)

I knew from an early age that I'd be an actress; it was simply an innate feeling. I didn't make a decision about it, it just happened. Deep down, I'm shy, but I learned how to conquer that to become an extremely outgoing person. I liked attention, and I could get it by performing in some way: getting up in front of a class, reciting a poem, reading an essay, even doing a jig or cutting up in class. And once I started working on plays, I could throw myself into the charac-ter—body, mind, and spirit; it was transforming. Naturally, at thirteen and dur-ing those first years with the Park Avenue Players, I was clueless about acting techniques. However, I learned a great deal just watching the others. Sometimes, in those situations, you learn more about what *not* to do, and that's valuable too. But the important thing is that we had a great deal of fun doing it all. We did staged readings and produced one-act and full-length plays, both on the stage in Phillips Hall and in the nave of the church. I worked for the Park Avenue Players for a couple of years, until I started a modeling career, and auditioning for profes-sional productions. That's when I really started learning about the *business* of show business.

Getting Started

There's great value in belonging to a theatrical company, even an amateur one. Many professional actors join a group when they're between engagements, and I learned much from the actors in the Park Avenue Players, especially how to seek theatrical jobs.

To set in motion a theatrical career there are two absolute necessities: professional headshots and a résumé. I found out who the popular photographers were, and when I was ready to start my theatrical preparations, I scheduled a photo session with James Kriegsman Sr., one of the prominent theatrical photographers of the time. (His son, James, Jr. has been taking my headshots for the past 20 years. When I find a good thing, I stick to it.) I also made up my first résumé by stretching the truth about all my work with the Park Avenue Players. It was true that I had appeared in *Ring Round the Moon, Everyman, I Remember Mama, Bell, Book & Candle, Family Portrait, Around the World in 80 Minutes,* and a long list of others; I simply omitted the church group association, and instead put them in the Off-Off Broadway category. My credits appeared more substantial that way. I then did research in a theatrical newspaper, *Show Business,* and made a file of all the agents and casting directors in the city so I could drop off my headshot at their offices. I also bought some spiffy audition clothes and comfortable flat shoes because I anticipated pounding a lot of pavement, as I made the rounds, going door to door. A few years later, another casting news publication, *Back Stage,* was on the stands, and we all rushed to buy the two papers weekly for their audition notices and articles about "the business," looking for any leads that might land us jobs.

I had recently graduated from high school and, with an attempt at practicality, went to NYU Business School for about half a minute. I decided almost immediately that I was destined to be an actor, and didn't want to waste any time, so I just stopped showing up at class. My mother gave me emotional support but I had to provide my own financial support, so it was necessary to get work that would generate a steady income. It had to be part-time work, at a place where I could get time off whenever I had to audition. I didn't want to work as an office temp, because I'd have to do the graveyard shift (midnight to 8 a.m.) in order to have my days free. Another choice was waitressing, but that didn't appeal to me since it seemed like too much toil with too little reward. It finally dawned on me that modeling would be the way to go. I was tall, very slim, photogenic, and people often asked me if I was a model, so it seemed the logical area to look for work, especially since my mother thought I'd be great at it.

Modeling turned out to be a really good idea; it even had the feeling of "show biz." I did some in-house modeling in the garment district, which was the least enjoyable. Besides, that turned out to be a nine-to-five job and that didn't give me the flexibility I needed. Usually there was one other model, and we had to be in the showroom throughout the day. When clients came in, we modeled the entire line for them. By the end of the day, we had dressed and undressed about fifty-five times. That was more tiring than being a waitress! Then I did some runway modeling, which was a bit like acting since there was music, an M.C., and an audience. Despite that, I couldn't get used to the awkward model's walk. You've probably seen them on television: Runway models are required to take long strides, crossing one leg over to the outside of the other—even describing it feels weird. If I stayed there too long, I figured eventually I'd end up in someone's lap in the first row.

I moved on to print modeling and that was the best of all three. A print model is paid by the hour so it's possible to make more money and, in the best of circumstances, it's the closest to acting. The model puts on clothes, assumes an attitude, and pretends to be someone else. The stylist makes everything perfect, the lights come up, the photographer starts clicking away, and the model is the center of the universe…for at least an hour. Naturally, it isn't always that wonderful. If it's catalogue work for a low-cost department store, the outfits are ordinary, the photographer snaps a few pictures, the model changes into the next outfit, and the next, and the next, in very short order. Still, it was exciting to be in a photographer's studio; the lights, cameras, and the scent of chemicals all held a fascination for me. And I liked the time spent with the photographers; they were more fun than designers and garment district manufacturers.

However, modeling was always a means to an end for me. I never liked it as much as acting. When I was on stage, nothing else existed, and I was transported into another world. It exhilarated me and put me in high spirits, and the feeling stayed with me for a long time. With modeling, when the session was over, I never thought about it again. Modeling jobs have the advantage of paying well, and that was important because I wanted to take as many acting classes as I could. I knew that raw talent and experience in a church group wasn't enough upon which to build a career. I always wanted to do my best in everything, and I knew that I had a lot to learn. In addition, modeling might help open some theatrical doors. But first, I needed to take classes, and I also needed to read as many plays as I could get my hands on. It's important for a young actor to understand the structure of a play and the development of a character, and that's best done by reading the work of great playwrights such as Shaw, Shakespeare, O'Neill, Williams, and Chekhov.

Initially, I studied with Thais Lawton who appeared in thirty-four Broadway shows, from *The School for Scandal* in 1909 to *The Romantic Mr. Dickens* in 1940. She retired from the stage and taught until she died in 1956. Then I worked with Lujah Fonnesbeck, a Swedish actress who taught in this country but never performed here. They're names no one would remember now, and frankly, nobody outside of show business really knew them in the mid-fifties, but they were excellent stage actresses from a bygone era. I never called them by their first names, so they were always Miss Lawton and Miss Fonnesbeck. I respected and looked up to these Grande Dames who had a theatricality about them which doesn't come from clothes or makeup, but from an attitude. They were stars, whether they were on stage or off. Both were from the old school of acting, so their approach was more from the outside in. They helped me tremendously with my voice, diction, and body language—all the external techniques. They encouraged me to see as many plays as I could afford, and that was an excellent learning ground. Ticket prices were low then: $2.40 to $5.40 for a matinee, and $3.60 to $8.05 for an evening performance. So if you had a few bucks in your pocket, you could usually see anything you desired.

There were many more straight plays (comedies and dramas) than musicals back then, which was good for me because that's what I was interested in. And by going to the theatre every week, I was able to observe a lot of actors. A play written at that time often had anywhere from twelve to seventeen actors in the cast. Today, the writer has to try to keep the cast down to four or five, or a producer doesn't want to touch the play—all those salaries would make it too expensive to produce.

I went to see the really good actors for inspiration. Their performances don't teach you *how* to do it, but they set a standard to attain, which is so essential. The acting couple of Alfred Lunt and Lynn Fontaine, always referred to as The Lunts, was perfection itself and I was mesmerized at every performance. Ruth Draper, the famous monologist, fascinated me with her characterizations. With just the placement of a large scarf, she went from a Scottish immigrant to a bag lady to three generations in one family. Other actresses that I was captivated by were the great Geraldine Page, Colleen Dewhurst, and Maureen Stapleton. Whenever they appeared, I made doubly sure I got a ticket as close to the stage as possible. Great performances can't be analyzed; the actors enthrall an audience for a few short hours, and the memory stays forever. Ah, but from the bad performances, one can learn how *not* to do it—that stands out like a sore thumb. In those days, I could, and would, sit through an entire performance, good or bad. Not now! I have no tolerance for bad plays or performances, so if it doesn't please me, I won't hiss or boo, but I will leave the theatre after the first act.

Once I learned the external acting techniques with Miss Lawton and Miss Fonnesbeck, I moved to a more realistic approach to acting by attending classes run by the popular teachers of the day. The old school emphasized the physical—voice, diction, body postures and movement. They broke down speeches by underlining certain key words, and never really thought about the emotions behind them, except in general terms like happy, sad, surprised, and angry. Nobody was acting in that fashion any longer, and hadn't been for some time, so it was imperative that I learn the present-day approach. One of my teachers was actor/director Jack Manning, who had first worked on Broadway with Helen Hayes in the play *Harriet,* and in later years, he created the Helen Hayes Shakespeare Company. I studied Shakespeare with Jack, who was able to combine style, voice, and realism all together.

My greatest teacher was Wynn Handman (director of the American Place Theatre—founded in 1963 by Wynn, Sidney Lanier, and Michael Tolan). We went to his studio on West 56th Street, across from the backstage of Carnegie Hall twice a week for four-hour sessions. Classes were small. We'd start the term with about sixteen students, and end with the ten or twelve who were really serious about the work. The technique he taught is what grounded me, and the one I continue to use. In this more realistic or truthful approach, everything is worked on from the inside out. We learned how to prepare for a part through emotional memory exercises, and improvisations. Wynn guided us into relaxation exercises, which helped us to focus and stay concentrated. We learned to listen and react truthfully and to trust our instincts. Through all the exercises, we developed freedom of expression. Scene work was the next step. We studied the characters from a psychological perspective, and were taught how to break down the actions and intentions of the character. There was a big sign in the room that said, "How can I give it, if it hasn't grown inside?" By using all the above techniques, and the magic phrase, "As If," the appropriate attitudes and feelings *did* grow inside.

"As If"—the use of this phrase can be explained very simply. Often an actor is called upon to react to something he hasn't ever experienced—a gun put to his head, losing a loved one, a decision to commit suicide—how can he react truth-

fully? By introducing the phrase "It's as if...." and then substituting something personal and meaningful to him. A gun to *my* head might be the thought of getting into an ice-cold shower. Insignificant to you, perhaps, but a fate worse than death for me. Of course, I don't just say the phrase; I explore all the thoughts, feelings, sensations, and memories that emerge in my imagination. Then when the gun is raised to my head, I don't have to fake the emotions, they'll all be there. However, if the cold shower idea was what I used in a scene, I'd never tell a soul. It all dissipates when it's talked about, so I always keep my choice a secret.

Studying acting is an on-going process that continues for years. At one point, I took classes from well-known directors, if they were giving workshops. When I was in my third Broadway show, *Nobody Loves an Albatross*, I took a workshop with influential director/critic/author Harold Clurman. I knew it would be a good learning experience. He'd been nominated for Best Director Tony Awards for *The Waltz of the Toreadors*, *Bus Stop*, *The Tiger at the Gates*, and *Pipe Dream*. I had read his book *The Fervent Years*, which was about his association with Lee Strasberg, Clifford Odets, Elia Kazan, and Cheryl Crawford, and their establishment of the Group Theatre in 1931, the most important theatre movement in this country. The book is a must for a serious actor or director. I had also read much of his theatre criticisms, and had seen some of the plays he'd directed. He was brilliant. Recently, I read a quote of his, which I love: "The stage is life, music, beautiful girls, legs, [and] breasts; not talk or intellectualism or dried up academics." I'm sure that the "legs and breasts" part was spoken with tongue in cheek since he was one of the great intellectuals of the theatre world, but he also had a great sense of humor. Years later, I worked with him, in his last professional association, at the Aspen Playwrights Conference in a John Ford Noonan play. (See the chapter on the Hampton Playhouse to learn what other work that intriguing workshop lead to.)

My acting mates and I took dance classes, too—not because we wanted to be dancers, but to get, and stay, in shape. I studied jazz dancing with Phil Black at the Carlos Dance Studios at 50th Street and Broadway, and also took modern dance at the New Dance Group Studio. I even bought some patent-leather Mary Janes with big taps, and tried tap classes, but the rat-a-tatting didn't appeal to me, so I stopped after about five classes.

One summer I enrolled in a New York University TV workshop with Clement Roberts. He taught us every element of producing a TV show: writing, acting, directing, lighting, and operating the cameras, but each of us concentrated on our main interest; mine, of course, was acting.

At the end of the semester, we all acted in scenes, which were transmitted to a theatre, to be viewed on a big screen by an invited audience. After the "broadcast," there was a critique by a panel of invited professionals, including a casting director from NBC. I performed a part in an original play called *The Land of the Midnight Sun,* written by a young man from Norway. About an hour before the performances, Roberts announced to the class that the actress who was to play a scene from *Antigone* was sick and would not be performing. He then asked me if I would fill in for her, so that her partner would be able to show off his work. I agreed to it, and God knows how I did it, but I memorized the part in that hour. It was just a fifteen-minute scene, but still it was daunting to do it with so little preparation—and no rehearsal. After our performances, there were comments by the panel, and the most memorable came from the NBC casting director, Martin Begley, brother of actor Ed Begley and uncle of Ed Begley, Jr., who commented on how good the actress was who played Antigone. Professor Roberts told him that I had just been given the part an hour before, and Mr. Begley responded, "Then I double my enthusiasm." I was flying high! This was praise from Caesar, and I was thrilled that I had taken that course.

About a month later, a secretary from the NBC office telephoned and said that Martin Begley wanted to speak with me. More excitement! When he got on the phone, he reminded me that he had seen me at the NYU workshop (as if I had forgotten!), and he complimented me again. Then he asked if I belonged to the actors' television union, AFTRA. I wasn't sure how to answer, and I thought that if I answered in the negative, I might not get a chance to do whatever he was calling me about. But in the flurry of excitement, I told the truth and said no. Fortunately, it turned out that was just the answer he wanted. They were looking for a non-union actress to work for an eight-week period while they trained executives in the use of the TV equipment in the event of a strike. (There were negotiations going on between the union and the networks, although a strike never took place.) A union actress would have cost them a large amount of money since we were to work an eight-hour day, and although I got a good salary, it wasn't union scale. They wanted to hire a small company, with a director who'd work with old TV drama scripts, directing the actors just as if it was going on the air. They kept renewing the eight-week contract and we all agreed to stay on. The other actors had all done professional stage work before but they were between-engagements and were pleased to have a steady income. The eight-week period turned out to be a full year, and it was a valuable learning experience for me—plus I got paid for it!

The year flew by, and when the job was over I missed going to the TV studio every day. I didn't fret over it though, because I wanted to land a part in a play as soon as possible. It was back to pounding the pavement. Making rounds is unquestionably hard work, but I was determined to get an agent, and I got right back into the swing of things. I sent out dozens of photos with an updated résumé to agents and casting directors. I also made phone calls and dropped by their offices, only to be told by the police (the frosty receptionists) that I couldn't be seen. I finally slid in through the back door. I had been freelancing with a few agencies as a model, and one day, I was asked to sign with the Dale Garrick Agency for Modeling. Luckily for me, it had a Theatrical and Television Department. Every once in a while, one of Garrick's TV agents would arrange an audition for me. They were usually for walk-ons or small parts, but that was okay. I just wanted to get my foot into the door—and I did! I got a number of *getting-your-foot-in-the-door* jobs. They were hardly acting jobs; they were more like modeling, with me in a bikini, or some other pretty and sexy costume. I decorated the stage on *The Garry Moore Show, The Tonight Show Starring Johnny Carson,* and a number of variety shows. On *Your Hit Parade,* I worked with Dorothy Collins in a musical number, "Queen of the Hop." We were on a basketball court, both in shorts, although mine were short shorts and I wore spiked heels. She wore ordinary sneakers, and was very frustrated because she couldn't get the ball into the extremely high hoop. The hoop on my side had been rigged to be just above my head, so when the ball came to my side, I would swing my hips to the beat and casually sink the ball. It was a delightful and amusing scene.

An actor can work on several TV shows without belonging to the union and then he's obliged to join. I didn't feel it was an obligation; I thought it was a privilege since it was exactly what I wanted, so I raced to the AFTRA office, plopped down the initiation fee and got my coveted AFTRA card. Belonging to the union doesn't get you work, but you can't work on TV without being a member, except for those first few shows. More important, it says that you're a professional, and agents and casting directors see you in a different light. I proudly put that card in my tote bag and said, "Look out world, I'm raring to go."

THE RITA ALLEN PRODUCTION
MILTON CASSEL & HARRY RIGBY

PRESENT

JUDITH EVELYN
MURRAY MATHESON   FRANCES ADLI

IN

SOPHOCLES'

"ELECTRA"

Adapted by FRANCIS FERGUSSON
Directed by DR. PATRICIA McILRATH

AND

"HARLEQUINADE"

A Farce
By TERENCE RATTIGAN
Directed by PHILIP BURTON

OFF-B'WAY FARCE. Marie Wallace is appearing in Terrence Rattigan's farce, "Harlequinade," at the Rita Allen Theatre. Also on the bill is Sophocles' "Electra."

SETTINGS BY
JOHN WARD

WITH
JOAN WETMORE

COSTUMES BY
AUDRÉ

LIGHTING BY
GARY SMITH

HAIR STYLES OF
RONALD DeMANN

CAST IN ORDER OF APPEARANCE
"ELECTRA"

Paidagogus.................NORMAN ROLAND	Chrysothemis..............JOAN WETMORE
Orestes...........................TOM BUCKLEY	Clytemnestra .... FRANCIS ADLER
Pylades.......................RICHARD HERD	Handmaiden ....JOAN CAMPBELL
Electra ....JUDITH EVELYN	Aegisthos..............MURRAY MATHESON

The entire action of the play occurs outside the Palace of Aegisthos.

"HARLEQUINADE"

Arthur Gosport.........MURRAY MATHESON	2nd Halberdier........ FRANK MONTALVO
Edna Selby .... JUDITH EVELYN	Miss Fishlock...... KATHLEEN ROLAND
Jeannie...........................MARCIA PAVIA	Muriel Palmer............ JOAN WETMORE
Dame Maud Gosport ......FRANCES ADLER	Tom Palmer.............. GRANT REDDICK
Jack Wakefield.............. EDWARD MOOR	Mrs. Burton...........JUSTINE JOHNSTON
George Chudleigh ....NORMAN ROLAND	Joyce Langland ....MARIE WALLACE
1st Halberdier.............. RICHARD HERD	Policeman .... WILLIS TOWNSEND
Fred Ingram ....TOM BUCKLEY	

The entire action of the play occurs between 6:30 and 7:30 p.m.
on a Monday in a Midlands town. Time: Recently

STAFF FOR RITA ALLEN THEATRE

Press Representative JOSEPH R. BURSTIN	Production Stage Mgr .. BOB LIVINGSTON
Assistant Press Rep......TED GOLDSMITH	Assistant Stage Mgr......GEORGE BORAS
Treasurer ....NATE MORGAN	Electrician .... ALBERT A. GORTA
Photographs........................DON LOOMIS	

Sophocles' *Electra & Harlequinade*

I discovered Greenwich Village while I was studying Shakespeare with acting coach Jack Manning at his studio on Bleecker Street. It was a quick ride from home on the Lexington Avenue IRT subway, and I was as fascinated with the Village neighborhood as I was with Shakespeare. It was truly old New York, with hidden streets such as Washington Mews and MacDougal Alley with their old lamplights and cobblestone streets, from which I could peek into centuries old houses. Washington Square Park was a fun place to stroll through, and scattered everywhere were coffeehouses, packed with poets and writers.

One morning, as I was almost out the door for another exploratory visit to the Village, my teacher telephoned to say that I should go to the Rita Allen Theatre at 120 Madison Avenue for an audition. He knew one of the directors, Patricia McIlrath, who was staging Francis Fergusson's adaptation of Sophocles' *Electra*. She had staged a production at the University of Missouri, Kansas City, the year before with Judith Evelyn in the title role. Evelyn was going to play Electra again, and the director had already cast the other principal roles. Now she was looking for six actresses for the Greek chorus. I got into a proper, serious, black outfit, and took the bus down to 30th Street and the 7 Arts Center where the theatre was housed. I did indeed get backstage…after I said, "Jack Manning sent me." I was given some sides (sheets containing the lines and cues for a single theatrical role), studied them right there, and was soon called up on stage. There were several people in the theatre, and I read for them. When I finished, a woman introduced herself as the director, and she asked if I belonged to the stage actors' union, Actors' Equity Association. I confidently responded in my best dulcet tones, "Yes, I belong to Equity, AFTRA and SAG." In reality, I was only in AFTRA, but being a member there had given me so much confidence, I felt it wouldn't be long before I belonged to all the unions. I was beginning to learn how to stretch the truth, because I knew that by adding all the other unions, much more importance would be given to the credits I had on my résumé. After all, every production I did at my church with the Park Avenue Players was listed as "Off-Off Broadway," and being a member of the union made the PAP appear to be a professional company. A little white lie at that point didn't bother me, because after all, if they didn't think I was good or right for the part, they wouldn't care what unions I belonged to. Conversely, if they liked me, it's possible that if they knew I didn't belong to the unions, they'd think I wasn't professional enough, and be afraid to take a chance on me.

After my interview with Miss McIlrath, I was introduced to the director of the second play, since it was to be a double-bill. That director was Philip Burton, a great Shakespearean scholar and the adoptive father of actor Richard Burton. He asked me to read for the part of the ingénue, Joyce Langland, in *Harlequinade*, written by Terence Rattigan, one of Britain's most important dramatists. Again I was given the sides, and after a few minutes went back on stage and read them. He chatted with me for a bit, thanked me, and I left the theatre. My next stop was the Drama Book Shop where I bought a copy of *Harlequinade* so that I'd be fully prepared for the next audition, assuming I'd have a callback. By late afternoon, I received a call and was told that, without the anticipated second audition, I was cast in the *Harlequinade* role and in the Greek chorus of *Electra*.

My plan had worked! The first thing I did the next morning was run over to Actors' Equity to join the union. Once an actor belongs to one union, he can join any of the others *if* he has a job offer. But I wanted to get there before the producers called, so that I'd be on record as a *member in good standing*. Looking back, I see how fortunate I was. Most young actors do an apprenticeship in summer stock for two years before they're eligible for an Equity card. That's not always a learning experience; unless you want to learn how to usher, run a box-office, clean up the lawn (at that time, mostly picking up cigarette butts), and paint scenery (the most fun, but not at 2 a.m.). Seems like cheap labor to me. Of course, if you're really lucky, you'll get a few walk-on parts and, if the gods are on your side, a small role. Admittedly, there are some first-rate summer theatres that run schools and give acting classes, and that's good, but I preferred my way.

Most important, I had taken a giant step forward—I was in my first professional stage production. My salary was about $35 a week, and I had to stop my modeling "Go Sees" (interviews), so I had a cut in my income for a while, but none of that mattered. I was on the boards, and on my way.

The first day of rehearsals arrived and I met all the producers, Milton Cassel, representatives from Rita Allen Productions, and Harry Rigby. Harry went on to produce twelve Broadway shows, from 1963's *The Ballad of the Sad Café* to 1977's *I Love My Wife* and 1979's *Sugar Babies*. I then was introduced to the wonderful cast of stars. First there was Judith Evelyn, who had become a star portraying Mrs. Manningham in *Angel Street*, a part she played on Broadway for three years. She followed that by playing the wife in *The Shrike*, and she appeared in many other Broadway vehicles. I discovered in an early conversation that she was an American, born in South Dakota, although I had always thought of her as Canadian, since she had done so much work there. Then there was Murray Matheson, who the *New York Times'* critic Brooks Atkinson said was "the spit and image of Cyril Ritchard," and he played comedy in the same stylish manner. (Ritchard was an extremely popular British actor and a beloved Captain Hook in 1954's *Peter Pan*) I learned a lot about comic timing just by watching Matheson, and talking with him, although admittedly, he was much better in farce than in Greek tragedy. Frances Adler, of the famous Adler acting family, played Clytemnestra. Her siblings, Luther and Stella Adler, were much bigger commercial stars, but Frances had remained in the Yiddish Theatre with her father, Jacob P. Adler, playing with such greats as Paul Muni, Jacob Ben-Ami, and Maurice Schwartz. Rounding off the star list as Chrysothemis was Joan Wetmore, an Australian actress who had extensive experience on both Broadway and in television. I was honored to be in such company in my first professional show. What a start!

Our three-and-a-half weeks of rehearsal flew by and my first professional opening night arrived: February 13, 1959. The evening opened with *Electra*, the classical Greek tragedy of the House of Agamemnon. It begins with the return of Electra's brother Orestes, who has come to avenge their father's murder. My entire family came that night, and they sat in Row A. When the lamenting chorus first appeared on stage, I could hear my sister, Margie, whispering, "Which one is Marie?" It took them a few minutes to figure it out, and then they settled down. After that, and forever more, I made sure that family and friends sat further back in the theatre. We in the chorus were very pleased when critic John McClain of the *New York Journal-American* wrote, "The mood of the piece is given strong impetus by a magnificently trained Greek chorus." And Brooks Atkinson said, "It is forcefully acted by Judith Evelyn and a company of players who know what they're doing…. The chorus has been imaginatively directed to comment on the story not only in measured speaking but also in dramatic movement that visualizes the development of the theme." Since he was the most important critic of the day that made me very happy indeed.

We followed the Greek tragedy with *Harlequinade*, a light farce about the backstage escapades of a touring company of actors rehearsing *Romeo and Juliet*. My character, Joyce Langland, is a young debutante who tries desperately throughout the play to get her boyfriend to leave the troupe. These days, nobody ever presents a Greek tragedy with another play, but Philip Burton said that the original productions in Greece always offered a comedy as a curtain raiser to warm up the audience. For some reason, Burton decided to do it the opposite way. Some of the critics didn't agree with the arrangement. Frank Aston of the *New York World-Telegram* wrote that *Harlequinade* "is a farcical peep backstage to set forth the cavalier argument that actors are slightly daffy in their complete interest in themselves…[but]…it surely would have been happier as a curtain raiser." He did like the performances and wrote, "Miss Evelyn is delightfully nonsensical and Mr. Matheson is merry indeed…[and] pleasant help is contributed by Marie Wallace." And we all liked the review by Robert Coleman of the *New York Mirror*: "We recommend *Electra* and *Harlequinade* to you. A versatile company does them justice. It could be the nucleus for a worthy repertory group—perhaps a United States replica of England's *Old Vic*. In our book, it has made an excellent beginning. It deserves the support and encouragement of thoughtful playgoers."

The arrangement of the plays worked well for the actors because *Electra* was highly stylized with the chorus in clown-white greasepaint—very mask-like. That makeup took a long time to put on but was easily taken off with Albolene (an unscented, moisturizing cream), and we could prepare for *Harlequinade* during the break, since for that we used natural street makeup. Our dressing room arrangement was very tight, with makeshift mirrors, and sometimes we had to move out of the room to get dressed, but the close proximity helped us to get to know each other very well.

During the run, I got my first call from agent Beverly Anderson, who worked at the Garrick Agency, my modeling reps. She talked to me about preliminary auditions for the much-talked-about upcoming musical *Gypsy,* based on the memoirs of Gypsy Rose Lee, a famous burlesque stripper. Ethel Merman was slated to star in the part of Rose, the quintessential stage mother of Gypsy. As exciting as that sounded, I paid very little attention to the call. After all, I was in serious theatre, chanting with the other five actresses in the chorus, and speaking with a British accent in a farce, so a mere Broadway musical didn't interest me—not yet, anyway.

We had a large cast and everyone got along quite well, just like in the Park Avenue Players, so I assumed every show would be like that. I learned as the years went by that it didn't always work out that way. Nevertheless, at the Rita Allen Theatre it was one big happy family. We were scheduled for a limited run, and although the reviews were favorable, they weren't *money* reviews, and it turned out to be a *very* limited run. We all promised to stay in touch but as so often happens, we didn't. However, I do have a life-long friend from that production, my longest show-biz friendship, and that's with Justine Johnston (Greek chorus and Mrs. Burton in *Harlequinade*). She's continued to work through the years, going from Broadway to television to the movies. I'll always remember her scene as Aunt Pearl in the 1981 film *Arthur,* when Dudley Moore staggers drunkenly into a restaurant and stops at her table. It's hilarious. She's since appeared on stage in fifty-one of the fifty-two United States (quite a feat), but unfortunately, we've never worked together again. That's almost always the case, unless you're in a repertory company or a TV soap opera, but happily we've remained good friends to this day.

The sad note was that we closed on Saturday, February 28, after only nineteen performances. It was a great experience, but in the theatre game of Life, I was back to Start. On the following Monday, I was ready to make rounds once more, but this time as a professional stage actress.

Marie with Carroll Jo
Towers, Faith Dane,
and Theda Nelson; and
above: with Ethel Merman

Gypsy

The upcoming Broadway show *Gypsy* was still being cast after *Electra & Harlequinade* closed, and I got another call from the same agent to audition for it. In some ways, being in a musical didn't really appeal to me; my mind was still into "serious theatre," and I thought I was very highbrow, still trying to keep the British accent that I had used in *Harlequinade*. But the reality was…I was out of work and wanted to be back on stage, and so I reacted differently to the second call. Besides, it was Broadway and work there would be another step up the ladder.

At first I was disappointed that I wasn't being summoned to read for a specific part. It was a chorus call for showgirls in a story about burlesque and legendary stripper Gypsy Rose Lee. What did I know about that world? But I like challenges, so an audition was arranged and I was told to wear rehearsal dance clothes that showed off my figure. At that point, I wasn't really sure what *rehearsal dance clothes* were, so I arrived at the Alvin Theatre wearing a bathing suit under my dress (most women weren't wearing slacks at that point).

If you've ever seen *A Chorus Line,* you know a bit about the audition process. We were all on stage in our dance clothes (I, in my bathing suit). The director kept eliminating performers until there were eight of us left on stage. At that point, he told us all to do the showgirl walk. *What was that?* I quickly looked around, got behind the most flamboyant of all the girls, and did a really good imitation of her. In fact, I went overboard and exaggerated all her movements. It worked and I got my first Broadway contract with a salary of $125 a week, a big jump from my last contract. The minimum payment for chorus work in 1959 was $103.50, but the agent who negotiated for the showgirls got us over twenty percent more than that. We paid her our ten percent commission and still were $9 ahead of the game—not exactly big-league, but at least we were up at bat.

It was exciting to contemplate being in the company of Jerome Robbins (director and choreographer), Arthur Laurents (author), Stephen Sondheim (lyrics), Jule Styne (music), David Merrick and Leland Hayward (producers), and the great Ethel Merman and Jack Klugman—not a bad roster of names for my first Broadway show.

Rehearsals were already in progress when I joined the company along with five other showgirls. The dancers and singers rehearsed in separate rooms from the scene rehearsals, and since the showgirls had just one big number at the end of the show, we mostly sat around in a room outside of the rehearsal rooms waiting for our turn. It would have been more exciting to watch the rehearsals in progress, but they kept us very compartmentalized. The upside was that the showgirls, Barbara London, Theda Meyers, Carroll Jo Towers, Gloria Kristy, Kathy Albertson, Denise McLaughlin, and I got to know each other very well. During a break in one of the rehearsals, Jule Styne sat around and talked with us. He said that he wrote the *Gypsy* score specifically for Merman; that it was like writing for a musical instrument, particularly the trumpet. And when you heard her sing, you could truly hear the trumpet sound. The air-conditioning in the room was up very high that day, and Jule asked me if I was cold. When I said I was, he took off his sweater and gave it to me. Later in the day, as he was leaving, I tried to return it to him, but he insisted that I keep it. It was a powder blue cardigan, snuggly and warm, and it was a fun memento to have from my first Broadway show.

Right through the sixties, productions almost always were taken on out-of-town tryouts for a few weeks before opening on Broadway. The shows would usually play in Philadelphia, New Haven, or Boston, and sometimes in all three cities. Many of the critics were well respected in those towns, and after the opening night reviews, the writers would frequently re-write scenes and songs. The cast and director would rehearse the changes each day and perform them at the evening's performance. It could be very hectic, but it was also exciting.

On the last day of rehearsals, before leaving for our out-of-town tryout, we had a "gypsy-run-through" of the show. These performances were traditionally done for all the other gypsies (actors/dancers/singers) who were appearing on Broadway, and anyone else involved with a production, plus friends and family. It was by invitation only. A notice would go to all the Broadway shows and it would be posted on the bulletin board backstage. My mother and a few friends came as my guests. It was a ritual at the time and was always very exciting. It was done on a bare stage, on the last Sunday afternoon of the rehearsal period, when the theatres were dark, since we played Monday through Saturday back then. ("Dark" is a term used in the theatre to indicate that there is no performance that day.)

I decided it was time to put on false eyelashes. I'd observed that some of the showgirls wore them all the time, and since we were going to be at the Winter Garden Theatre (one of the largest stages in New York), without any stage lights,

I truly needed them. I bought a set at the Makeup Center (a professional makeup store where most actors bought their makeup) and attempted to put them on without cutting and shaping them. In retrospect, I looked more like Tammy Fay Baker than a sexy showgirl until one of the more seasoned showgirls came along, took pity on me and removed them, trimmed them to fit, and glued them back on.

There were no sets or costumes at the run-through. The singers wore regular street clothes and the dancers and showgirls wore rehearsal clothes. By then I had the proper outfit, which was a leotard, but instead of plain black, I chose to wear purple, just to be different. For music, there were just two pianos, a bass, and drums, and yet it was pure magic. It was especially exhilarating when Baby June and Baby Louise (played by Jacqueline Mayro and Karen Moore) were singing "Let Us Entertain You," and from the back of the theatre, Ethel Merman made her entrance by shouting, "Sing out, Louise," and then she pranced down the aisle and up onto the stage. It brought the house down, and we were only five minutes into the show.

There were a couple of showstoppers like that throughout the performance. In fact, when the three featured strippers (Maria Karnilova as Tessie Tura—later Golde in *Fiddler on the Roof,* Faith Dane as Mazeppa, and Chotze Foley as Electra) did "You Gotta Have a Gimmick," the audience went wild, and there were three reprises at that performance. The song's premise is that if a stripper just bumps and grinds, and even "pulls all the stops out, 'til they call the cops out," she's not going to go very far unless she has a gimmick, too. Electra got rich by "doing it with a switch," Tessie Tura did it with finesse (as a ballet prima donna), and Mazeppa bumped it with a trumpet. Actually, the song wasn't written until after they hired Faith Dane who auditioned doing bumps and grinds playing "The Call to the Post," the trumpet music played just before a horserace. She knocked them out with her audition, and they hired her without actually having a number for her. Somewhere between that audition and the start of rehearsals, the number was written. It was a clever, funny, unique number, and although all the gimmicks were good, the trumpet was the best.

All the showgirls were in a big Christmas number toward the end of the show. In the actual production, there was a huge flat (an oblong piece of wood covered with canvas and painted) that reached to the top of the stage, in the shape of a Christmas tree. At the end of each branch was a singer or dancer dressed as a Christmas decoration. On the sides, at floor level, the "presents" came rolling out on tracks with the showgirls in scant costumes, hats, and garlands, and that's where I was. My outfit consisted of two balls and a reindeer strategically placed, and a huge bell on my head. At the run-through, we just had the bare stage and the audience's imagination. As the number came to its conclusion, we took Christmas decorations in the form of Styrofoam balls and threw them out to the audience, and they loved it. That was the only performance where we threw out the balls, and I wonder if those who caught our offerings, kept them. They'd be great collector's items. It was a thrilling afternoon, and to this day, I'm sure anyone who was in that house remembers it vividly.

Monday was spent packing and preparing to leave for Philadelphia, and on Tuesday we were on our way. The train trip from New York to Philly was an education in itself—all three hours of it. Faith Dane was very outspoken, just like her stage character, and she loudly and proudly exclaimed that the last time she went to Philadelphia, it was to have an abortion. Her bluntness was a bit shocking to me at the time, yet it was so out of the blue that it was funny, too. Besides, I never knew if she made up all those outrageous stories, or if they were true. (It was probably a little of both.)

Over the next few days, everything—costumes, sets and music—fell together. Up to that point, there was just a rehearsal pianist (John Kander) for the musical numbers. Then, on the third day, the entire orchestra appeared. To hear Stephen Sondheim's lyrics, and Jule Styne's music, with all the brass, strings, woodwinds, and every other instrument that makes up a show orchestra, was so exciting that it brought me to tears. As far as I'm concerned, the entire score is great, and the overture is my all-time favorite—"Curtain up, light the lights, we've got nothing to reach but the heights"—what could be better than that?

We opened at Philadelphia's Shubert Theatre in April of 1959, and played to packed houses every night. During our time in Philly, the director tried cutting the Christmas number several times. The show was running too long and it wasn't something that helped advance the story, although it was quite spectacular. We showgirls would check in at the theatre at *half-hour* (half an hour before curtain time), and when the curtain went up at 8:30 p.m., we would be dismissed if the number was cut. One evening, as we were walking around town, we saw our producer, David Merrick, and he expressed surprise at seeing us there and not in the theatre. We told him what was happening and he said that he'd make sure our number stayed in the show. It was never cut again during our Philadelphia run.

Toward the end of our engagement in that city, we had a photo call, a session arranged with professional photographers who snapped us as we went through the motions of a performance. These photos would be used in the souvenir program, ads, posters, and in front of the theatre. The most popular show photographers for many years were Friedman & Abeles, and they were there to do our session. Photo calls are traditionally done after an evening show, and we followed that custom. Union rules mandated that we had to have a meal break, which the producers catered and served backstage. Then the photo shoot began. Since the show ended at 11 p.m., we started the first shot around midnight. The session went on through the night and into the wee small hours of the morning. At 5 a.m., we were still there—most of us exhausted, practically sleeping on the floor, even though we showgirls were just hanging out, since we were only in the one big production number at the end of the show. On the other hand, La Merman was full of her usual vim and vigor, and not simply posing for the pictures but still belting out her songs. She had more energy than anyone did in that theatre. No wonder she could belt out a high C on demand and be heard in the last row of the balcony, and without a mike! Hundreds of photos were taken that night and I've included some of the showgirl shots here.

We had a successful six weeks in Philadelphia and the audiences would have come for months more, but New York and an empty theatre were waiting for us, so we packed up and headed to the Great White Way.

We did two previews at the Broadway Theatre in New York; the first one on May 19 (my birthday), and it was the best birthday present I could get. The opening was on May 21, and the audiences loved it. Merman knocked them out with her tour de force "Rose's Turn," which came at the end of the show. It was awesome. Many said Merman's performance was one of the great events in musical stage history.

We settled into our New York run and found we showgirls had lots of time backstage since we didn't appear on stage until Act II. Faith Dane (Mazeppa) started to do some marvelous oil paintings during the lengthy wait. Before long, we were all bringing in paints, brushes, and canvases, and testing our talents with a paintbrush. There were at least fourteen of us sharing one big dressing room, and instead of the usual smell of grease paint, the overwhelming scent in the air was turpentine and oil paints. At one point, when I couldn't find anything around our room to paint, I just made myself up as a clown, propped up my canvas in front of the mirror, and proceeded to paint my face. The stage manager happened to stop by that night, and he had a fit when he saw me. But I knew I had enough time to take off the clown makeup, and apply my glamour makeup before we went on, so I tried to reassure him that I'd be ready. He wasn't quite convinced and told me not to do that again. Next time, I painted a nude from a clay model, but somehow I wasn't getting the backside right. One of the girls,

Theda, who had a perfect backside, insisted I copy hers, so she'd pose in front of me, in her scanty costume, until I got it right.

We produced over a hundred paintings, and when Seymour Krawitz, the publicist for the show, saw our studio, he decided that we had to have an art show. And we did indeed—at Junior's Backyard (a restaurant/bar where all the musicians hung out, next to the entrance of our theatre on 53rd Street, with a backyard that was adjacent to our backstage alley). I displayed six of my paintings. Ethel Merman bought two paintings at the opening show and both of them were mine—"Blue Vase with Flowers" and "Stone God." She loved the colors in my work, most especially the purple flowers surrounding the statue in "Stone God" (purple was her favorite color). Merman's parents were introduced to me a few months later at a local restaurant, and it pleased me to hear that she had given them a gift of my paintings, and that they were very happy with them in their home. I was very proud about my sale, and when the show at Junior's closed, it moved on to Macy's, where another of my flower paintings was sold. We brought in quite a few dollars with that show, and the proceeds went to the Actors' Fund organization.

Lots of craziness, fun, parties, and bonding were part of the Gypsy experience; learning to paint backstage, forming a softball team and playing against other gypsies and *Playboy* Bunnies every Thursday afternoon, canoe races in the Hudson River, and an endless stream of publicity pictures—petting animals, feeding lions, falling out of canoes, always smiling our biggest smiles…whatever the publicist thought would make a good picture and stir more interest in the show by making the local newspapers. At that time, publicists always followed the principle of the three B's of publicity—Babies, Beauties, and Beasts—and we chorus gals fell nicely into that category. In *Gypsy*, it was the showgirls they wanted for the publicity shots, so it was Barbara, Theda, Gloria, Carroll Jo, and I who were photographed the most.

I'll never forget one particular publicity event: a canoe race on the north end of the Hudson River in upper Manhattan. It was Barbara, Theda, and I (clad in bikinis) against the girls in *Flower Drum Song*. They didn't have a chance! We had gone up to the club a week earlier and were trained in how to maneuver the canoe, and we picked up the technique quickly. We were confident that we'd win, but we made a pact that if we got a little behind, we'd overturn our boat and get the attention of all the photographers. As luck would have it, we started off on the wrong foot, or the wrong *side* as it turned out. As we picked up our paddles and in unison said, "Left," Carroll Jo put her paddle into the water on the right side. Barbara and I tried to compensate by quickly switching to the right, but by then C.J. had changed over to the left. You've got the picture—we were going in circles. We were laughing hysterically, but we did get the canoe straightened out and were heading for the dock when we saw that the little *flower-drummers* were fast approaching the finish, and all the photographers had their cameras aimed their way. We knew it was "man-overboard-time," and the next thing we knew we were in the water. Naturally, the cameras focused on us, and Barbara and I swam to the dock. Carroll Jo thought she'd be more dramatic and accepted a life preserver that was thrown to her from an anchored yacht. It turned out that our idea was better, since she was too far away to be photographed (although she met some interesting men on board). Needless to say, all the photos in the newspapers were of us, overturning, swimming in, and saving ourselves. We were interviewed for the papers and some radio shows, posed for lots of pictures, and then, when one photographer told us he had missed the shot of us in the water, we just jumped back in and reenacted it.

The Broadway Show League is a softball league made up of performers and stagehands from a variety of Broadway and some Off-Broadway shows. Since I was a tomboy as a kid and loved sports, it was only natural that I join the *Gypsy* team when it was forming. Men and women didn't play on the same teams then, so we had a separate women's league. The men were the really serious players, but every Thursday that year and the next, the crowds came to see The Girls of *Gypsy* on the field in Central Park at 63rd Street, and we played some interesting teams. *Flower Drum Song* had a team, and their captain was Keye Luke (a well-known film and TV actor whose career spanned sixty years). Actors Studio had another team, but (perhaps expectedly) the biggest crowds came out when we played the *Playboy* Bunnies. Even though we didn't play as well as the guys, we threw ourselves into the game with gusto, and gave the fans a good show—sliding into base, throwing our bats, having temper tantrums, and climbing the fences—sometimes to catch a ball, but just as often to pose for a photographer. For all that, some of our teammates played very well. (Marsha Rivers was our captain and pitcher and she was an ace player.) And while it was all done in the spirit of fun, it was always a challenge and we played to win. I did stop short of hurting myself, except once, when I was playing in the shortstop position. To catch a line drive, I put up my right hand (instead of the one with the glove) and I fractured my pinky. It was a clean break, a hairline fracture, and I just wore a little silver splint on it, which I decorated with the trimmings from my costume. As Pollyanna does, I always turn a negative (in this case, a splint on a broken bone) into a positive (another pretty and decorative thing on my finger).

Merman was a pro when it came to her work and was pleasant to everyone, but she definitely wasn't very chummy with the chorus kids. I doubt if she knew one of our names. I figured that out around Christmastime, almost three quarters of a year after we'd been together. The stage manager asked us all to come down and line up outside of Merman's dressing room. We all did and he directed us to go into her room one at a time. As we entered, he read off each name. She in turn plunked a package in our arms and said, "Merry Christmas" and repeated the name. We thought from the size of the box that it was champagne but instead it was inexpensive cologne. It was a little impersonal, but at least she had the holiday spirit.

On the Memorial Day weekend of the next year, four of us had the pleasure of working with Jimmy Durante, the star I had seen at St. Catherine's Irish Night when I was nine years old. He was doing the nightclub circuit at that time, and he traveled with his own musicians, but not showgirls, although they were always written into the act. Most clubs had a group of dancers or showgirls he could use, and he had a choreographer who would visit the club in advance, pick out four girls and teach them the act. But this particular weekend, he was to appear at the Concord Hotel in the Catskills, and they didn't have a chorus line. It was arranged for his choreographer to come backstage to meet us, and she picked Barbara, Marsha, Theda, and me to work with Durante. It was for one night only (Sunday, our dark night), but it was a wonderful experience. We were driven up early Sunday morning, and when we checked into our rooms, we found a message that we'd rehearse with Durante later in the afternoon. At the rehearsal hall, introductions were made, and within five minutes I felt as though I'd known him for a long time; he had such a warm and friendly personality. He ran quickly through the routines with us, and we were then dismissed until show time. That evening we were assigned to a good-sized dressing room, and after a few minutes Durante came in to wish us good luck. When he looked around our dressing room, he said that it was much more comfortable than the one they had given him, and asked would we mind sharing it with him. Needless to say, we were delighted. At one point, he asked us how much we were to be paid for the evening's work. When we told him, he said, "That's not enough. We'll give you each $50 more." When I was talking to one of his musicians, I found out that although his long-time drummer had been sick for quite a while and hadn't been able to play, he continued to pay him his weekly salary. He was a truly generous man, and I'm glad I got to work with him, as brief as it was.

We went back to New York on a bus at 2:30 p.m. the next day, and the trip that usually takes two hours took more than five! It was the end of the Labor Day weekend and everybody was making an exodus out of the mountains. We had a show in New York that night and nervously watched the traffic jams, but miraculously we arrived at Port Authority Bus Station at 7:30 p.m. Because of the traffic jams at that hour, we thought running from 42nd Street to 53rd Street would be faster than a cab, and we arrived at our backstage entrance at exactly 8 p.m.—our check-in time (half-hour).

Counting rehearsals, out-of-town tryouts, and the run at the Broadway Theatre, I was with the show for a year-and-a-half. It actually ran for seven more months, for a total of 702 performances, but with a five-week break in between. On July 9, 1960, because of a contractual agreement *Gypsy* closed so that Merman could have a vacation. I'm sure that clause began when there was no air-conditioning in theatres and she continued the tradition throughout the years. Unfortunately, due to the complicated and expensive costumes and set, and six additional chorus girls, the Christmas number was dropped when it reopened at the Imperial Theatre on August 15. I managed to save a picture, and have included it in this book. As far as I know, the Christmas number was never used again in any production of *Gypsy*.

It was a remarkable learning experience, being around all that talent, and absorbing everything. Actor Eli Wallach once said that an actor has to be a great big sponge, soaking up everything life throws his way. All those experiences go into our storehouse of memories, waiting to be called upon when we create a character.

I learned discipline, the importance of cooperation, promptness, preparedness, and teamwork (all the attributes of a professional), during the run of *Gypsy*. What's more, having that nice long run gave me the opportunity to study acting very seriously. Happily, I made many good friends, and two of those friendships—Barbara London and Theda Nelson—have lasted a lifetime. All in all, I wasn't sorry that I gave up my British accent for that first taste of Broadway.

The original
final production
number in *Gypsy*

Wedding Bells

At a very early age, I met Gregory Lewis Pollock, the man who was to become my husband. I wasn't yet twenty-one when Greg and I were introduced. He was quite a few years older than I, but that didn't matter; we were attracted to each other immediately. I was dating a few other men at that time, but after our first meeting, I stopped seeing them all and spent every evening with Greg. He became my greatest fan and supporter.

One of the things Greg and I had in common was a love of the theatre. He was a plastic surgeon and had many theatrical patients and friends, but his attraction to show business started many years before he became a doctor. As a teenager in New York City, he appeared in movies as an extra, just so he could be around the movie scene. It was easy to get to the Astoria studio, just a bike ride across the Queensboro Bridge. The fourteen-acre complex is still very active with sound stages, TV studios (*Sesame Street* has been filming there for the past ten years), music-recording studios, the American Museum of the Moving Image, and a fourteen-theatre cinema. Greg told me that he enjoyed doing that for a couple of years, until he worked on a film in which he had to be in a sword fight with the star, John Barrymore. I guess Barrymore didn't like how Greg was getting the best of him in the duel, so he lost his temper and tried to stab Greg in the chest for real! Greg decided then and there that he'd had enough of that part of show biz. After giving up acting, Greg worked as a piano player in several New York nightclubs. He was a good musician and knew lots of popular music, so it wasn't difficult to find steady work. While he was working in the clubs, during the day he was still going to college, then to medical school. When he got his medical degree, he had to get serious, so he put away his sheet music and left show business for good. He went to Germany to study with some of the most prominent plastic surgeons of the era. He didn't want to be a general surgeon—he was interested in being around the Beautiful People, so he turned to plastic surgery. He loved his profession, and it kept him in close contact with the theatrical scene because so many of his clients were in show biz. So were his wives! He was married and divorced twice before we met. His first wife was a dancer, and the next was a singer. I suppose it was only fitting that his third and final wife be an actress.

We met through a press agent named Joe Russell. I was modeling at the annual Automobile Show at the Coliseum, the main convention center in New York at the time, located at 59th Street and Columbus Circle. (It's been demolished since then and New York's first upscale shopping mall is there now in the Time Warner Center.) Joe was doing press for the show and one evening he invited me out for a bite to eat. He said he was with a friend who was parked outside in a black Cadillac, and that after dinner they'd drive me home. It had been a long workday, and food and some relaxation sounded like a good idea.

It was easy enough to find that distinctive car and there they were, inside it. Joe jumped out of the passenger seat and I slid in as Joe climbed into the back seat and introduced us. Greg and I immediately got into a conversation, somehow excluding Joe. Mostly we talked about show business and me, since he kept asking me questions about my interests. We were heading downtown and when we reached 47th Street, Joe announced that he'd like to get out there. I had thought earlier that all three of us would go to a restaurant, yet I didn't mind that he was leaving. I was attracted to Greg's straightforward personality and I wanted to get to know him better. Being alone together was an appealing idea. After we said our good-byes to Joe, Greg asked if I was in the mood for an ice-cream sundae or an alcoholic drink. I chose the latter, figuring that's what he'd want. He told me months later that he really expected me to say, "ice-cream sundae." We headed uptown and over to Madison Avenue where Greg knew a quiet neighborhood restaurant on the corner of 69th Street. We had a drink and light supper and we talked for a long time—it was as if I had known him for years. We could have talked through the night, but he had an early morning operation scheduled so we decided to leave around 10:30 p.m. He drove me home, gave me his business card, and said that if I'd like to see him again, I should call. That was an unusual approach. At such a moment, it seems like most men just ask for your phone number, which can put you in an awkward position if you aren't interested. But he was cool, and I liked that, so the next day I did call, and accidentally asked for Gregory *Peck* instead of Pollock. I guess I was nervous about the call, but because I was calling his office, the secretary knew who I meant. Greg and I chatted for a few minutes and made a date for that night, and the rest is history. From then on, for the rest of his life, there was never a day that I didn't see him, except when I was out of town with a show, and even then we spoke on the telephone every night.

My birthday, May 19th, was just ten days after our first meeting. He asked me in advance if I'd like a watch as a present. I said I would, indeed. I hadn't owned a watch up to that point, and I assumed he'd buy me a nice, little, inexpensive Bulova watch. (I heard the ads on radio and television for years, "America runs on Bulova time," and I was brainwashed.) It was a great surprise to me when I opened the box and found a beautiful diamond watch. I cherished that watch, and on our wedding day, he presented me with a diamond band to complete the look.

Within the year, we got officially engaged. This time his gift was a spectacular four-carat diamond ring with smaller diamonds on each side and set in platinum. As a kid, I had always looked longingly into jewelry store windows at the three-carat solitaires, daydreaming that the man of my dreams was putting it on my finger. Greg went one carat better, and I preferred his choice to the one in my fantasy. We didn't want to wait much longer so we zeroed in on July 29th of the following year as the date for the wedding.

I went to Bergdorf Goodman and had my gown designed. I always longed to be different, so instead of the traditional full-skirted gown, I decided on a long sheath (straight skirt). The bridal assistant came up with a great design—a fitted bodice with an oval neckline that had an inch of pearls around the edge, three-quarter sleeves, and a straight skirt with a detachable train (shades of the removable peplum from my grammar school graduation). It was to be made up in an elegant satin peau-de-soi material, and because of the detachable train, would be extremely versatile. For the dinner party, the train could be hooked up around my waist, turning it into a bustle, making it very practical for dancing. When leaving the party, it could be used as a cape. I love change of all kind, and even my wedding gown couldn't just have one look for the evening.

A friend from my *Gypsy* days, Theda Nelson, made my headpiece and veil. She's a marvelous artist and eventually became a textile designer. We went shopping in the bridal area of the Garment District—between 34th and 40th Streets, from Fifth to Ninth Avenues—and by the end of the day, my mind reeled from the amount and variety of veils we saw. I let her make the final choices of veils and pearls and she put it together beautifully. Theda constructed the headpiece with a certain hairdo in mind, so she also joined me and my mother, father, and maid of honor in our hotel suite on *the* day, and made all the finishing touches.

We were married at a landmark Fifth Avenue hotel, The Sherry-Netherland, at 59th Street, across from the main entrance to Central Park. Greg was Jewish and I was Protestant, and although we wanted a spiritual service, neither of us wanted to be married in the other one's church or synagogue. We definitely didn't want a civil ceremony by a judge. That would be too cold. We decided to have a Society of Ethical Culture leader officiate at the wedding. Ethical Culture is a humanistic religious movement that's bound together by a belief in the dignity of each person and a commitment to help create a better world. That appealed to both of us, and it turned out to be the perfect ceremony for us.

For my entrance down the stairs to the chapel, I had on my full outfit with the traditional train, and a veil covering my face. I walked down the aisle with my father, and as we reached the front of the chapel, Diddy (my dad's nickname) just turned away and sat down next to Mom, forgetting to lift the veil. (I've seen so many weddings where that happens—I guess the poor fathers are more nervous than the bride.) In any event, my maid of honor, Dolly Martin, somehow managed her flowers and mine and lifted my veil, and we proceeded. Greg was able to say his vows loud and clear, sounding like an actor, while I kept fighting back tears, hardly getting the words out. The ceremony was followed by a cocktail reception and then an elegant dinner party and dance. It was a fabulous wedding celebration with two hundred of my friends and family. Everyone had a good time but I think I enjoyed it more than anyone.

It was great living with someone who was not in the same profession, yet who had such an affinity toward it. Often I'd bring home a script, study it and then ask Greg to run the lines with me. He'd read all the other parts while I tried a variety of approaches with my character. Sometimes he gave me directions, and sometimes I even took them. But mostly it was the encouragement along the way that I liked. He supported me just as my mother had done, making me feel that it didn't matter how many auditions I lost, that there would be more coming up and I was bound to win the next, or the one after that. So thanks to Greg's support, I almost never lost my self-confidence or got discouraged. If I did, he'd cheer me up in such a way that I'd approach the next audition feeling on top of the world. There were times when he'd drive me to an audition and wait for me (he still had that big, baaaaad, black Cadillac), and we'd both take pleasure in the moment if I came out of the theatre waving the script in the air. That meant I either had a callback, or I got the part. Either way we'd celebrate. And of course he was just as supportive if I came out empty-handed.

I kept auditioning and it wasn't long after Greg and I were married that I got my first acting role on Broadway (Hallelujah! I was out of the chorus), and I knew that was a good sign. It was the delicious role of Roxana in *The Beauty Part*, which you'll read about in the next chapter. Greg always came to see my shows several times, and when he didn't attend a performance but was just coming to pick me up, if he could park his car, he'd often come in toward the final fifteen minutes and watch the performance until the end. Sometimes, he looked like a Stage-door Johnny hanging out backstage, kibitzing with the doormen until the show was over and I joined him. I'm happy to say, he was around during all of the Broadway, Off-Broadway, Summer Theatre, and television shows that I did in the sixties (you'll read about them in the upcoming chapters). From time to time, he chauffeured some of the cast and me to the theatre, or took us to the beach on our days off, or gave us some worldly advice; but always, he was in my corner cheering for me.

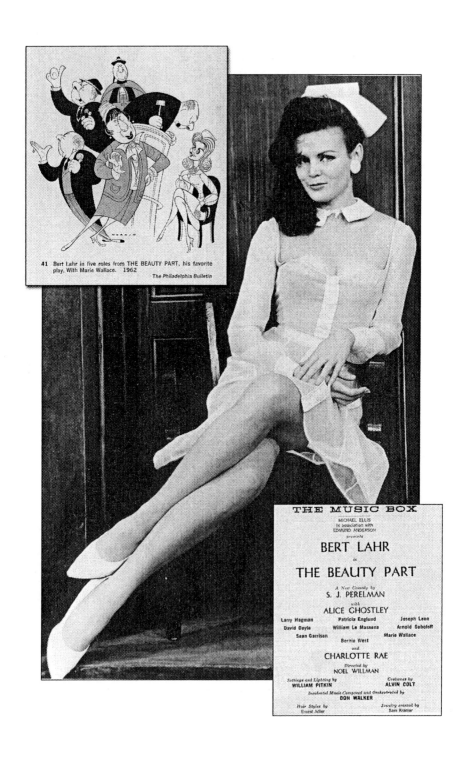

41 Bert Lahr in five roles from THE BEAUTY PART, his favorite
    play, With Marie Wallace. 1962

The Philadelphia Bulletin

THE MUSIC BOX

MICHAEL ELLIS
In association with
EDMUND ANDERSON

presents

BERT LAHR

in

THE BEAUTY PART

A New Comedy by

S. J. PERELMAN

with

ALICE GHOSTLEY

Larry Hagman	Patricia Englund	Joseph Leon
David Doyle	William Le Massena	Arnold Soboloff
Sean Garrison	Bernie West	Marie Wallace

and

CHARLOTTE RAE

Directed by
NOEL WILLMAN

Settings and Lighting by   Costumes by
WILLIAM PITKIN   ALVIN COLT

Incidental Music Composed and Orchestrated by
DON WALKER

Hair Styles by   Jewelry created by
Ernest Adler   Sam Kramer

That's *The Beauty Part*

Life gives you lots of little lessons, and I've gotten plenty of them during my show-biz years. One thing I learned early on was that losing an audition didn't mean that I was unsuccessful. First and foremost, I always ask myself the question, "Did I accomplish what I set out to do?" The goal is not simply to get the job, although that's certainly a big part of it. It's more important to prepare myself both physically and emotionally to be the best I can be at that particular moment; to be completely relaxed; to make strong choices; and to have clear objectives as the character, and then to go after them as fully as I can, not worrying what *they* want from the reading. If I get all that, I feel I've accomplished a great deal.

I also learned that I might not get a particular job even when I've done all of the above, and everyone at the reading *loves* me. Here's a perfect example: When I was in my first professional show, *Electra & Harlequinade*, I auditioned for a refrigerator commercial. Those were the days when television auditions were in front of *live* producers, directors, and account executives (not in a casting director's studio, facing a video camera, as they are now). In any event, the audition went very well and I had a "callback" for it. (A callback is just what it sounds like—when an actor is asked to come in for a second reading of a part, after an initial one.) The second audition was also good but I didn't get the booking. I was young enough to think, "They didn't like me," or, "They found someone better," or any number of negative things. About four years later, I got a call from a producer named Edmund Anderson who was in pre-production with another producer, Michael Ellis, for a new Broadway play, and he asked me to come in to read for a part. When I met him, he told me that he was the account executive on the refrigerator commercial I didn't get, and that he and his wife had come to see me in my play at that time. He further explained that I didn't get the spot for one small reason…they were all afraid that I was too glamorous and would overshadow their product! At the same time he told himself that if he ever produced a play, he'd make sure I'd have a chance to audition for it. So, here was the play and a part I was right for. I auditioned for him, and then for the highly regarded director/actor, Noel Willman (he had staged *A Man for All Seasons* earlier that year and I had been extremely impressed by his work). My new agent, Michael Hartig, called soon after that with word that I had a callback a few days later. I wore the same clothes and combed my hair exactly the same as the first audition and went to the theatre with my well-studied script. When I finished reading, the other producer, Michael Ellis, came up on stage, and talked about starting dates and asked about my availability. As we said our good-byes, Ellis added that he'd speak with my agent later. He made it sound like I had the part, and I was pretty excited, but I tried to remain cool. I knew that until I heard from my agent, and I actually signed the contract, nothing was definite. I agree with legendary film producer, Sam Goldwyn, who often said, "A spoken contract isn't worth the paper it's written on." My union's rulebook states the same, but in slightly different words.

I didn't have to wait too long, and by the end of the day, my agent called to break the news that I landed a part in my second Broadway show, S. J. Perelman's *The Beauty Part*. That was a great lesson for me: Don't assume the obvious because it's almost never true. Besides, things always work out for the best, if you just sit back and wait…and keep working somewhere else.

Perelman's title for the play was taken from a phrase that only a New Yorker says and understands. One critic even said at the end of his review that although he liked the play, he still didn't know the meaning of "the beauty part." Perelman once described it to us as "a Brooklyn colloquialism—one that a counterman in a hamburger stand might use. He'd say, 'The job doesn't pay much and the hours are long, but the beauty part is that I can eat all I want on the cuff.'"

On the morning of October 29, 1962, we had our first rehearsal. It was held at a studio above Ratner's, a famous kosher dairy restaurant down on Second Avenue and Ninth Street. Since the restaurant was just below us, we often went there at lunchtime, and that's where I learned to eat and love bagels, blintzes, and borscht. Before that, I couldn't have told you the difference between a bagel and a blini.

Everyone involved in a production is at that first rehearsal, so the first hour was spent making introductions over coffee with my fellow actors, director, writer, producers, and all the production staff. It wasn't a musical, but there was to be incidental music between scenes, so the composer/orchestrator, Don Walker, was there, as was the musical director, Abba Bogin. I was delighted to see my old friend from the Park Avenue Players, William Pitkin, who had signed on as Lighting and Scenic Designer; otherwise, everyone was new to me. The director assembled a brilliant cast, and heading it was Bert Lahr (a known name in burlesque and vaudeville before making his Broadway bow in 1927 in *Delmar's*

Revels, followed by dozens of appearances on the Broadway stage, and his most famous role: the Cowardly Lion in the 1939 film classic *The Wizard of Oz*). He played seven different characters starting with Milo Leotard Allardyce DuPlessis Weatherwax. Larry Hagman played Lance Weatherwax, his idealistic son who was in search of self-expression. It was pretty early on in Larry's career, and he was best known, at that time, for being Mary Martin's son, since Ms. Martin was the superstar at that point, and everyone knew her. Not too long after that, he began to have great success with his television show *I Dream of Jeannie* and later, as the dastardly villain J.R. Ewing on *Dallas*. Then, of course, the tables turned, and Mary Martin was often referred to as Larry Hagman's mother. It seems to mean the same thing, but in terms of notoriety, it makes a world of difference.

Our director, Noel, advised us to try to invest the "nutty" world of S.J. Perelman with a "total logic." He said that he wanted it to be funny but that he didn't want it to be "only funny," that audiences would get as sick of that as they would a play that was only pathetic or only tragic. He also said that we should develop "a kind of arrogance about the play so that if the audience doesn't get a joke you go right on as if there were plenty more where that one came from." He added that it must be played "as lightly, as truly, as deeply, and as swiftly as possible."

We spent the rest of the morning taking care of Actors' Equity business—signing all our insurance papers and information sheets; talking about the play, sets and costume designs; and voting for a company deputy. The deputy is the liaison between the actors, theatre management, and our union, and, also, the person who handles any backstage problems that might come up. The cast overwhelmingly picked me, and I was honored. Little did I know that no one ever wanted that job, and they always tried to enlist the most inexperienced actor, meaning the one who didn't know enough to say "No!" It's actually a very important position, and it shouldn't be handled so carelessly. However, it turned out to be okay because one of the cast members, David Doyle (a very experienced Broadway actor, and later known as Bosley on the hit TV show *Charlie's Angels*), agreed to be *my assistant*. In any event, things ran smoothly from that point on, except for one time, out of town, when there was no heat backstage on a Thursday night. Management wasn't too swift in rectifying the problem, and by Saturday, it was very cold. Since it was the weekend, I thought I'd have to wait until Monday (a business day) to call Equity, but David suggested I call immediately, and sure enough, a representative called me back within a few minutes, and the problem was fixed without any further delay. I gained a little extra experience that I hadn't counted on, and since I ran to David about everything, I got to know him very well, which was an extra-added pleasure, because he was always good for a laugh, and when he had a few drinks after the show, he was outrageously funny.

The last rehearsal week was spent at the New Amsterdam Roof at 214 West 42nd Street, in Times Square. It was a former theatre/nightclub, dating back to the glamorous heydays of Florenz Ziegfeld, where there were midnight shows after performances of *The Ziegfeld Follies* (1913-27) downstairs in the New Amsterdam Theatre. By 1962, it was a gloomy rehearsal space, accessible by riding up a wheezy elevator. Bert Lahr was the only one in our group who had played at the theatre in its heyday, and it saddened him to see its condition. Today, the Disney Corporation owns the building, and the theatre has been completely reconstructed. Since 1998 *The Lion King* has been playing there. We merely had a big, cold, dreary room with folding chairs, but we managed to get through that last week and were ready for the road.

The Beauty Part had out-of-town tryouts for one week in New Haven, Connecticut, at the Shubert Theatre, and at Philadelphia's New Locust Theatre for three weeks. The play had its New York premiere at the Music Box on West 45th Street, opening a day after Christmas. Three weeks before that, the nine New York daily newspapers had been shut down by a printers' strike so the critics' reviews didn't get printed. They were good reviews, with great quotes for the ads, such as:

"[*The Beauty Part*] is an epic of sorts—all sorts. Written in Latin, Yiddish, and various other kinds of English…two things work in its favor, it's against integrity, and it's funny."—Walter Kerr, *Herald Tribune*

"Lahr and Perelman make happy music together."—Howard Taubman, *The New York Times*

"Excruciatingly funny. They gave me my best Christmas present…. S.J. Perelman conceived it and he had it delivered by Bert Lahr and some other extremely hilarious people. There are very comical assists by Larry Hagman, David Doyle, and a towering red-head named Marie Wallace."—John McClain, *Journal American*

All of these reviews were sent to the press representative of the show, so we did see them in print, so to speak. And many of the reviewers read them on radio and television news shows, but that wasn't the usual practice, as it is today, so very few people heard them, and consequently, the show remained an exceptionally well-kept secret.

It's a wonderful play, not surprisingly, since Perelman was one of the best humorists of the twentieth century. He wrote many books, was a regular contributor to the *New Yorker*, went to Hollywood in the early 1930's, and wrote screenplays for the Marx Brothers—*Monkey Business* and *Horse Feathers*. Another film assignment was *Around the World in 80 Days,* and that brought him an Academy Award. He collaborated on some Broadway musicals, notably with Ogden Nash and Kurt Weill on *One Touch of Venus* in 1943, starring Mary Martin, but he'd never written a straight (non-musical) stage play. His characters and their names, full of puns and wordplays, were always outrageous, never more so than in *The Beauty Part*. Perelman once described the play to us as "a spoof on the current itch to be creative, lampooning culture-conscious America."

Another of Bert's characters in *The Beauty Part* was Hyacinth Beddoes Laffoon, a female publisher of a chain of pulp magazines, completely adorned in a Chanel suit and turban, bedecked with jewels, silk stockings, and high heels. Some of the other actors, playing a variety of roles, were Charlotte Rae (later Mrs. Garrett on TV's *Facts of Life*), Alice Ghostley (*Bewitched, Designing Women*), Arnold Soboloff, Joseph Leon, William La Massena, and Fiddle Viracola. Everyone, including many reviewers, thought Perelman had made up Fiddle's name too, but that was, and is, her actual name.

My character was Roxana DeVilbiss, an unlicensed masseuse, and I had to appear before Judge Herman J. Rinderbrust, played in the best burlesque style by Lahr. Being a Perelman creation, it was in a mock courtroom in a TV studio. Today we have many TV courtroom dramas, but in the sixties, that was a unique concept. It was a truly funny scene, and I wish Broadway productions had been videotaped in those days, because *The Beauty Part* and its original cast were brilliant, and every aspiring actor should be able to see and study it.

As Roxana, I wore a transparent dress, beautifully designed by Alvin Colt. It was extremely short in length, and low cut in the bodice, but with a little pique collar around my neck, to make me appear pseudo-demure. I also wore a nurse's cap perched very smartly on my long red hair, and four-inch heels. At one point during the run, someone in the wardrobe department washed the dress and put it in a dryer, and it shrunk up to the size of a doll's dress. (It wasn't too big to begin with!) They stretched, pressed, pulled, and stretched it again, and my full five-foot-nine-inch body was finally able to fit into it, barely, and I wore it that way for the rest of the run. It may have even been better than the original...I told you...everything always works out for the best.

I learned several lessons from Bert during the run of the show. One was how to conserve your energy. When I wasn't on stage, I'd watch the show from the wings on stage left, where Bert made one of his entrances. The first few times I saw him coming slowly up the stairs from his basement dressing room, with two stage managers assisting him, I wondered how he could possibly play his next scene. He would then stand slumped against the wall, waiting for his cue to enter. He was playing that wonderful character, Hyacinth Beddoes Laffoon. On cue, he would straighten up, dance across the stage, and trill "Good morning, good morning, good morning!" to his six male flunkies. He would then leap up onto the desk and continue a most hilarious scene. Lesson learned: He wasn't tired, or sick, or too old to perform; he was just saving all his energy so that he could *explode* on stage. I found that to be quite remarkable.

The other lesson I learned wasn't as pleasant for me. However, it did teach me something about comedy. My part was small, but delicious, and I was responsible for one good laugh. It would happen after Judge Herman J. Rinderbrust (Lahr) said to the jury that he wanted them to look at this "sweet, pure, innocent child." I immediately did a movement exactly opposite to his words; I licked my lips, thrust my body forward, and gave a most lascivious, come-hither look. The audience loved it, but Bert had more to say, and was working up to *his* laugh. He couldn't figure out why they laughed at that point, (he was above me and leaning forward in his judge's bench). Well, each night he inched his way back, and finally saw my little shtick. Next day, there was a matinee, and I had to pass his dressing room to get to mine. He called out to me, "Marie, darling, I want to talk to you, come in here." I did, and he said, "You know, darling, you mustn't ever move on another actor's line." I knew what was coming, but I played innocent (always stay in character!), and asked what he meant. When he told me, I replied that Noel, the director, knew I was playing it that way, and that I'd done it all through our out-of-town tryouts. Bert didn't care. He agreed that it was cute, and I was getting a laugh, but he was working on a really *big* laugh, and mine ruined that for him. I was so mad because it was my moment, my laugh. However, when I went to Perry Bruskin, the stage manager, he told me I had to listen to Bert. It slowly dawned on me that Bert was right; one big laugh *is* much better than a few small ones, but it sure was disappointing to me back then. I'd be less than truthful if I didn't tell you that I did sneak it in whenever he wasn't looking my way, and I enjoyed the audience's laughter once again.

Promoting a new Broadway production without the metropolitan daily papers is almost impossible, and *The Beauty Part* was one of the first new productions to feel the pinch of New York's newspaper strike. It truly hurt our mail-order ticket sales, which made up about fifty percent of theatre business at that time. We also had to move the show from The Music Box because Gertrude Berg was scheduled to open in The Theatre Guild's production of *Dear Me, The Sky is Falling*. The producers felt that we had to stay on 45th Street in order for potential ticket buyers to find us. We went into the Plymouth Theatre, as a last-minute interim booking, to keep it on the same street. It would have been a great theatre for us, but the drawback was that we could only have it for three weeks since a new Lillian Hellman play, *My Mother, My Father and Me*, was booked for March. We went on a week-to-week basis at that point, and hoped that another theatre on 45th would become vacant. It didn't, and the producers finally decided to close it on March 9th. We played to a packed house that last night, with thunderous applause, and we all cried on stage as we sang, "Auld Lang Syne," believing that we could have run forever with that kind of audience response.

Our production didn't have a very long run, only 85 performances, and it made us all very sad to close, but those who saw it remember it as one of the highlights of that Broadway season. I surely enjoyed almost every moment of its run, and as in every show I've ever been in, I came away with another life-long friend, Fiddle Viracola. And that's *The Beauty Part!*

Constance Ford, Robert Preston, and Marie.
Above: with Leslye Hunter.

PHILIP ROSE and ELLIOT MARTIN present

ROBERT PRESTON
in

NOBODY LOVES
AN ALBATROSS

A New Comedy by RONALD ALEXANDER

with CAROL ROSSEN

PHIL LEEDS   AUSLEY WINTER   FRANK CAMPANELLA
RICHARD MULLIGAN   BARNARD HUGHES   MAXIE WALLACE

MARIAN WINTERS   LEON JANNEY   CONSTANCE FORD

directed by GENE SAKS

Scenery and Lighting by WILL STEVEN ARMSTRONG
Costumes by FLORENCE KLOTZ

LYCEUM THEATRE
149 West 45th Street, New York City

Everybody Loved the *Albatross*

Robert Preston gave me the confidence to win the part in my next show. I was entering the backstage area for my callback for *Nobody Loves An Albatross* at the same time that the show's leading man, Mr. Preston, was going in. He was so friendly: greeting me, chatting with me, and finally wishing me "Good Luck." Wow! I was flying. I felt as if it were an omen. I was prepared for the reading and already pretty sure of myself, but now I knew I could do no wrong.

My first audition for the show had happened a few days before, with the director, Gene Saks, who had started directing on Broadway with 1963's *Enter Laughing* (he'd been a marvelous, and very funny performer before that, and he continues to wear both hats). The *Albatross* author, Ronald Alexander, who was famous for his play and movie *Time Out For Ginger* was also there, as were the producers, Philip Rose and Elliot Martin. In stage productions, the director has the final say in casting, though if the star is big enough, he or she will have a lot of input. This is unlike TV, where the producer and/or the lead writer are often in that power position. But often in theatre it's a collaborative effort, with the writer, director, producer, and star in agreement. I knew there must have been a few discussions between the first and second auditions. At this point, they were going to make their final decision.

I read my scene on stage with the stage manager, while my judges sat in the darkened house. I went home feeling quite positive, told Greg about it, and then dropped the subject—until I got the hoped-for call from my agent, Michael Hartig, with the good word that I was cast in the role of Linda. My third Broadway show! That was cause for Greg and me to celebrate, as we always did when something good happened. Actually, we painted the town often, but this was extra special.

Within a week, the company began rehearsals, and again as I ascended the stairs to the rehearsal hall, there was Robert Preston, who said, "Welcome aboard!" He always made everyone feel so comfortable. He was already a superstar; he had appeared in more than thirty movies in Hollywood since 1938, and on Broadway he had starred in eleven productions, including 1957's *The Music Man* in which he delivered one of the all-time great stage performances as con man "Professor" Harold Hill. However, you always felt he was simply part of the team; he never played "star." Indeed, on the first day of rehearsals, he gave an informal speech to the director and actors saying that he was just another member of the cast and he expected to be treated as such. He was a great guy, or as we'd say in New York, a *mensch*. I've worked with many stars since then, but my two all-time favorites are Robert Preston and Gwen Verdon. (I'll tell you more about Gwen in a later chapter.)

Rehearsals began and I discovered the many other wonderful actors who were in the show. It was a time in the theatre when plays had large casts, and what a cast it was: Richard Mulligan (who went on to great fame playing Burt Campbell in the 1970s TV series *Soap*); Frank Campanella; Carol Rossen; Marian Winters; Barnard Hughes (who played in hundreds of stage, film, and TV productions including a short stint on *Dark Shadows* in 1966); Phil Leeds; Leslye Hunter; Jack Bittner; Gertrude Jeanette (who later became an award-winning playwright and director, winning the 2002 Paul Robeson Award); Leon Janney; Constance Ford (star of many Hollywood movies, who played matriarch Ada Downs on NBC's *Another World* from 1964-89); and of course, Robert Preston, or Pres, as we all called him.

The usual Equity business was conducted in the morning, and then we took a lunch break. I went to a nearby restaurant with Pres, Connie Ford, and Marian Winters. I had to leave about fifteen minutes early to run to my agent's office to sign my contract. In all the excitement of getting another part, I had forgotten to do that very important thing. (Remember, I'm the one who doesn't believe she's in a play 'til the contract is signed.) I slipped Connie $20 and asked her to put it toward my share of the lunch. When I got back to the rehearsal hall, she gave me back the cash, saying that Pres had treated us to lunch. In my most recent Broadway show, the star didn't even give the traditional opening night presents, just one telegram to the entire cast, so our first day luncheon treat was an unexpected pleasure and just the beginning of the generosity Pres showed throughout the run.

As is usual for a Broadway-bound play, the rehearsals lasted three-and-a-half weeks. The last days before leaving for our out-of-town tryouts arrived. On November 22, we were at the rehearsal hall (again, above Ratner's), and spirits were high. There was the customary ten-minute break after working for two hours (a union rule), and I stopped in the office for a cup of coffee. The TV set was on, tuned to CBS: *As the World Turns*.

Suddenly the world was turned upside down. There was an interruption in the program with an unbelievable announcement by news anchorman Walter Cronkite. President Kennedy had been shot. Within minutes, the entire cast was in that tiny office, stunned and speechless, trying to make sense out of the total confusion. Rehearsals were stopped, of course, and we all stayed glued to the TV. But there wasn't enough space for all of us in that tiny room, so the entire cast went to the local Chinese restaurant, where there was a big TV set. We were all in shock, as was the world. It was devastating, and I've felt nothing like it until I experienced the September 11 attacks. The moments are seared into my memory. There was anger too, but against whom? Who had committed this ghastly act? We cried uncontrollably, until we were numb, but we didn't want to leave. We just clung to each other and, at one point, held hands and prayed. We finally separated after many hours, and I went home to Greg, and then *we* were glued to the TV set for the next three days.

The three main television networks did continuous news coverage right up to and including the funeral. And so much happened during that time. Lee Harvey Oswald was arrested for killing a police officer and within five hours was charged with assassinating President Kennedy. As Oswald was being transferred from a Dallas city jail to a county jail, nightclub owner Jack Ruby shot and killed him, with dozens of cameras capturing the event. It was the first time in TV history that a murder was seen live. It was hard to believe our eyes. How could the police have allowed that to happen? There were so many questions: Did Oswald act alone? Was the Mob behind it? Or the CIA? Some even asked, did Lyndon Johnson have anything to do with it? To this day, after all the inquiries and commissions, there are some people for whom these questions still haven't been answered satisfactorily. And back then, nothing else held any importance for us. Radio stations either had news or played funereal music, sporting events were cancelled for the weekend, Broadway shows were dark—all our normal activities came to a halt. On the Sunday after the assassination, November 25, at 11 a.m., the most solemn funeral procession began, led by Jackie with her two children and her brothers-in-law, Robert and Edward Kennedy. They went from the White House to St. Matthew's Cathedral, where there was five minutes of silence, which was observed across the country and probably around the world. Our country's "one, brief, shining moment" (Camelot) was over.

But life goes on, and so does the theatre. We had one more rehearsal, and then took off for Connecticut. The Shubert Theatre in New Haven was our destination. Most shows stayed there for only a few performances, and that's what we did, as planned. Our next move was to Boston's Wilbur Theatre, where we played for three weeks. That gave us two out-of-town opening nights, and Pres was again so gracious, sending us all lovely wishes and presents of champagne and flowers.

During our first week in Boston, I ran into Connie Ford one morning on her way to the beauty shop to get her hair washed and set, which seemed like a perfectly good idea, since we didn't have a show hairdresser. But the next day, I saw her again, and she was going to the same place for a comb-out. Why would she go so often, I asked. She said she had gotten so used to Hollywood, and everyone taking care of her, that she'd forgotten how to fix her own hair. That seemed extravagant to me, so I said that whenever she needed help, to call me. The next night, I heard her scream up the stairs, "Help!!!" and I went to her rescue. I styled her hair for that evening's performance, and for many after that, and I think my handiwork looked even better than the beautician's.

Connie had been greatly affected by the Kennedy assassination and most especially with Jackie's reaction to it. She kept a framed picture of Jackie in the dressing room, referring to her as her hero. There wasn't a time when I was there that she didn't talk about her. Of course, we talked about other things and even had a few laughs together. But mainly, we were preparing to go on stage, and when I finished her hair, I ran back to my dressing room to finish my own hair and makeup.

About a week after we got back to New York, Connie bought me a present of an Emilio Pucci blue silk jersey shirt. (Pucci was famous for his use of brilliant colors and featherweight jersey shirts and dresses, which you could take straight out of your handbag to wear.) She said it was to show her appreciation for all the work that I had done with her hair. The shirt was beautiful, and I loved it, but it was quite unexpected, since it wasn't hard work for me. I just considered it a delightful way to get to know her better. She was, as Jackie Gleason would have said, a great dame. (I know that's what he'd say because I got to know him well later, during my work with him in *Sly Fox*. He had a manner of speech that some women would have been offended by, but it didn't bother me. I know that it came from a certain era when colorful slang was used freely and lovingly, and when he called *me* "a great dame," I was flattered.)

Connie's part in *Albatross* was actually a "tribute" to another great Hollywood dame, Lucille Ball. Lucy, by then already a legend for *I Love Lucy*, was starring in her second sitcom, *The Lucy Show*, at the time *Albatross* opened, and had recently purchased Desilu Studios from her ex, Desi Arnaz. Connie's part was that of a tough but funny comedienne, starring in her own hit sitcom, and owner of a studio. The resemblance wasn't so coincidental when you knew that the playwright,

Ron Alexander, had spent several years in Hollywood working for Desilu Studios. But at the time, I knew none of that.

Albatross was originally written in three acts. My scene was in Act Two, Scene One, and during the last days of the three previews in New York, they tried it as a two-act play, ending the first act with my scene. It worked so much better that the director and writer decided to keep it that way. I've always preferred two acts, or even just one long act. But for many years everyone followed the same formula: The first act was mostly exposition; it set up the whole story, and it was usually not too long. The second act was always the longest, because that's when the plot unfolded. And the third act tied everything up. But in the 1960s, many playwrights changed to the two-act formula, and we were among the first to do it.

The action took place in Beverly Hills, in the living room of Nathaniel Bentley, a charming, charismatic, fast-talking, opportunistic movie producer, played by Pres. My character, Linda, was a high-class hooker, hired by Bentley for the evening. I had what turned out to be one of the funniest lines in the play. Here's the set-up: I rang the doorbell, and Nat opened the door. I didn't introduce myself, nor say a word to him, although we had never met before. He looked at me and then at his twelve-year-old daughter, who was sitting on a hassock at right center stage, and he said to me, "You can wait in the other room." I then made a long cross from stage left to stage right, constantly looking at the young girl. The audience knew exactly who I was and what I was there for, by the way I was dressed, and just as I opened the door to the other room, my shawl slipped off my shoulders, and I looked over my shoulder at him and, very flatly, said, "I hope that's your daughter." It brought the house down.

If I were playing in the show presently, I wouldn't describe the action of my scene. There's something about saying out loud that a piece of stage business works and is funny, that has quite the opposite effect on it. In fact, when we were in Boston, Ronnie (the author) came to me and said that he loved the way my shawl slipped off my shoulders just as I spoke my line—that the timing was perfect. That did it! For the next few performances, it didn't work. Either I was too conscious of it, or I was working for the laugh, or I tried to make it happen—I don't know—but I do know that it killed it for a while. I got over it by the third day and it all came back and was again one of the biggest laughs in the show.

One of the other things Ronnie told me that day was that they auditioned more actresses for my role than for any other part in the show. He said they saw one beautiful actress after the other, and they all looked great, but none of them could be funny. It was my comedic sense that cinched the part for me. That pleased me enough that I didn't get angry at him for screwing up my line. (He'd call it *his* line, but once I do a part I take ownership.)

Our Broadway opening was at the Lyceum Theatre on December 19, 1963, and sure enough, bountiful, beautiful bouquets of flowers were waiting for all the actors in our dressing rooms. But more significantly, Pres wrote a very personal note to each of us. To me, he wrote, "I see you so briefly, but I enjoy it so much." It was a simple note, but I found it so touching. I'm not a sentimentalist, so I don't keep a great deal of memorabilia, but that card remains in my makeup kit to this day.

The play was well received, and the most influential critic of all, Howard Taubman of the *New York Times*, called it "a hilarious comedy with a slashing satirical edge. Preston is giving a marvelous, sustained performance as a prize con man…[and] is a formidable joy. Gene Saks has directed an excellent company in a hard, punching style…. And let's not forget Marie Wallace as an impressively constructed caller." Along the same lines, I got a big kick out of an item in Robert Sylvester's syndicated column. It went like this: "Two fellows [in the audience] at *Nobody Loves an Albatross* were admiring stunning Marie Wallace, who plays a call girl in the comedy. 'Is that what a Hollywood call girl really looks like?' demanded one. 'Only if they're lucky,' said his more sophisticated friend."

In June of 1964, Pres left the show; he had only signed on for a six-month period. Barry Nelson replaced him, and he was excellent in the part, although very different. (He had a softer approach, and was less cunning and manipulative.) We played for a while longer, and then the closing notice went up. On June 20, after 212 performances, we packed it in. It was a great crew and I enjoyed my relationship with all the actors. I never worked with any of them again, although Connie and I saw each other a lot when our TV shows shared a huge studio in Brooklyn five or six years later. That's when I was in *Somerset*, which you'll read about in a later chapter. I saw all the shows that Pres did after that, visiting him backstage afterwards, and he continued to be one of the most delightful men I have known.

I was lucky enough to have another show to go into immediately following the closing, so I wasn't too disappointed. It was a great run while it lasted, and I'm happy to say that everybody loved that *Albatross*.

Segue into *Angel Street*

Auditions for *Angel Street* were being held while *Nobody Loves an Albatross* was still playing at the Lyceum Theatre, and my agent, Michael, arranged an audition for me. I deliberated about whether I should try out for it, as I was already in a Broadway show, and the new contract would just be for a summer regional theatre production. However, it was a nice part, and would be a good addition to my résumé. I also realized that no decision had to be made unless I was offered the part, so I might as well audition and take it from there. I only had to read once for the director, Peter Waldron, and on Monday of the following week, I did get the offer. The only drawback was that it was a two-week engagement, and rehearsals were to begin in less than twelve days.

At that point in June, I figured *Albatross* would run through the summer, so I thought I could do both. My idea was to get a leave of absence from *Albatross* for those two weeks, and let my understudy, Beverly Penberthy (Pat Randolph, *Another World,* 1967-82) take over during that time. Then as soon as *Angel Street* closed, I would go back to my Broadway role. I went to discuss it with one of the producers, Philip Rose, but the closing notice for *Albatross* went up before he had to make a decision. (According to Actors' Equity rules, a closing notice must be posted on the backstage bulletin board by the last performance of the previous week, in order to close at the end of the next week.) On June 12, I signed the contract for the new show; *Albatross* closed on the 20th, and *Angel Street* rehearsals began on Tuesday, the 23rd. Fast work! If only every period "between engagements" during my career would be that short....

Our producers were Hal Thompson and Jack Anderson, operating at The Theatre in Westchester, located in Dobbs Ferry, N.Y., a summer stock theatre that featured a new star and production every week. We had an interesting cast. Sylvia Sidney played the lead role of Mrs. Manningham. (Sylvia started her career on the stage and graduated to the movies with a part in *Broadway Lights* in 1927. She became a Hollywood star in 1931, when she replaced Clara Bow in *City Streets.*) Kent Smith—a Broadway, Hollywood, and TV actor—played her husband. (His first role in New York was as the juvenile lead opposite Clark Gable in David Belasco's *Blind Window*, but the play closed before reaching Broadway. His real debut was in *Dodsworth* in 1934 playing Fay Bainter's lover. From that point on, he constantly commuted between New York and Hollywood.) Woody Romoff, a wonderful character actor, was cast as a detective. Ethel Remey played Elizabeth. She had the role of the Reno innkeeper in the original Broadway production of *The Women*—a play in which I was to have a major role many years later.

We quickly got through our introductions and Equity business and began a whirlwind rehearsal period; we had just six days to prepare the play and on the seventh day, we would open. This thriller by Patrick Hamilton is probably more familiar as *Gaslight*, the 1944 film classic that starred Ingrid Bergman and Charles Boyer. In the film, Angela Lansbury played Nancy, the tarty housemaid with a cockney accent. (That was my part in our stage production.) Interestingly enough, Judith Evelyn, my old friend from *Electra*, had played Mrs. Manningham in the first Broadway production of *Angel Street* many years before. The play is typical melodrama, with a diabolical husband who methodically attempts to torment, menace, and drive his wife mad. It's an ominous plot and was great fun to work on, especially since I wasn't the woman driven to near insanity.

Opening night came and went very quickly, and we had seven more performances to go. Since the theatre wasn't far from the city, we all commuted there daily. If Greg were free, he'd drive up, see the last part of the show, and drive us home. He loved to talk with Sylvia and Kent about old movies, all of which he'd seen. Those trips were as much fun as the play itself.

I shared a dressing room at the theatre with Sylvia and her three pugs (ugh!). She didn't go anywhere without them. She had previously been married to the great actor Luther Adler, and it seemed that he raised pugs, or at least had lots of them, and sold some to Sylvia. Well, those pugs made themselves at home in our dressing room, and most especially on my side, and often in my costume. The dogs were the love of her life, so I always had to be very careful not to disturb her pets. I had one costume and, for some reason, they loved it, and occasionally they got a little too comfortable on it. One night, one of those "adorable" creatures mistook my dress for a litter box, and I must say, I drew the line there. I won't say I blew my top, but I made sure that could never happen again. The stage manager divided the room in half with the help of several screens, and the pugs never crossed my path again. I seem to remember that we were very subtle in our explanation to Sylvia, convincing her that she needed some privacy, and wouldn't it be nice to have one whole area all to herself and her darling pugs?

I had seen Sylvia Sidney and Kent Smith in movies over the years, and now I had a chance to act with them, and that was a real treat for me. Nothing much more eventful than the naughty dogs happened in that run, and it was a short, but pleasurable experience. However, another door opened when the Dobbs Ferry door closed, and it led me to the Hampton Playhouse.

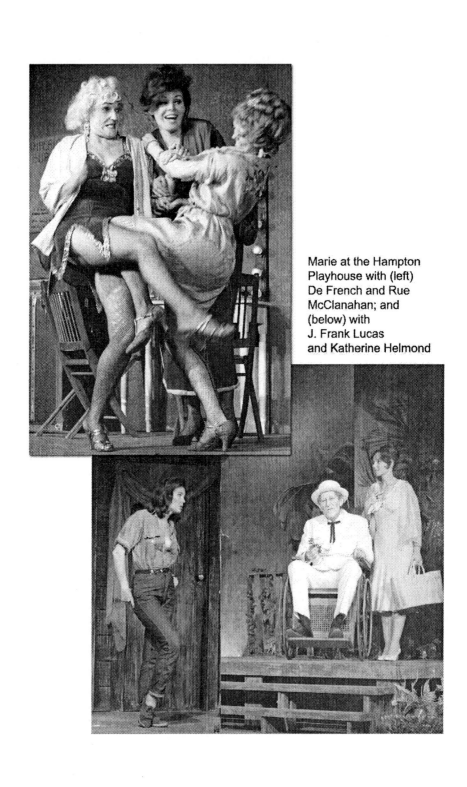

Marie at the Hampton
Playhouse with (left)
De French and Rue
McClanahan; and
(below) with
J. Frank Lucas
and Katherine Helmond

The Hampton Playhouse

The Hampton Playhouse

The Hampton Playhouse

The Hampton Playhouse

It's fitting that I repeat the name Hampton Playhouse, since it was the summer theatre I returned to over the years, loving every minute. It was truly a unique place, managed by producer/director Alfred Christie and producer/actor John Vari. I had the opportunity to play so many diverse parts there with a great number of gifted actors. The best actors in New York always played the Hampton Playhouse at least once (Grayson Hall of *Dark Shadows* worked there in 1963), and many made the trip from the West Coast to appear at the theatre. It was summed up succinctly in the introduction to *Behind the Stage Door...an Inside Look at 50 years of the Hampton Playhouse*, a 1997 book about Al and John written by their business manager, Bobby Stockbridge. In the introduction, editor Ann Carnaby wrote, "The Hampton Playhouse should be on a register of fabulous institutions known for nurturing love, talent, self-confidence, artistic endeavor, acceptance and incredible respect for one's self and one's fellow [actors]."

Chance got me there. During the run of *Nobody Loves an Albatross,* I attended Harold Clurman's workshop, which I wrote about in "Getting Started." It was held in a Carnegie Hall studio at 11:30 at night. Starting time for Broadway musicals in 1964 was 8:30 p.m., and 8:40 p.m. for a straight play, with the curtain usually coming down a few minutes before 11 p.m. The timing of Clurman's workshop was perfect for those of us in Broadway shows because we were able to come directly to class after our curtain calls. Professional directors made up the rest of the class. Clurman often suggested scenes to the directors, and they'd cast the parts from among the actors in the group. One of the directors was Alfred Christie, and he asked me to work on S. N. Behrman's *Amphitryon 38* with actor John Vari. It's a stylish and funny play about the god Jupiter's love for a mortal, Alkmena (that's me). In our scene, Mercury (John) comes to Earth to sketch out Jupiter's love for Alkmena and prepare her for his visit. It was fun exploring the roles, and getting to know Al and John. It was then that I found out they were the managing directors of the Hampton Playhouse, a two-hundred-year-old barn-turned-theatre in New Hampshire, and that they would be leaving in a few months for their summer season.

The three of us rehearsed in John and Al's apartment and brought our work to the next meeting of the group. Clurman gave brilliant directorial notes, which we incorporated into the scene at our next rehearsal. He always insisted that the actor be very specific about his choices, and once made, to follow through completely. He said the choice didn't matter; that the important thing was to embrace it fully, to be totally committed to it. That was great acting advice. When we felt we were ready, we presented the scene to the class once again. It went well, and I then started on another scene with a different director. (That part was Josie Hogan in *A Moon for the Misbegotten*, a part I loved, and one I worked on in another class with Wynn Handman. I'm sorry that I never got to do a full production of it. Josie is one of my favorite characters, a towering Irish earth mother who suggests the warrior women of the Celtic race.)

Fast-forward a few months, to the beginning of the summer, when I received a call from Alfred. They had a small problem: They had cast actress/writer/comedienne Renee Taylor (later Fran's flamboyant mother on TV's *The Nanny*) in three of the plays that summer, and at the last minute, she got a movie assignment and couldn't do the plays. Was I available? It just so happened that I was working in *Angel Street,* but it was scheduled to close before the Hampton rehearsals would begin. Once more, I was (ironically) delighted that a show was closing. I jumped at the chance to work at the Playhouse, and within two weeks, I was in Hampton, N. H., settled in my little motel room with kitchen privileges, directly across from the theatre on Winnacunnet Road, ready to begin rehearsals on July 21 in Tennessee Williams' *The Night of the Iguana,* playing the part of Maxine. At that point, I was a bit young for the role, but it was a great stretch, and I had the good fortune to work with marvelous people.

Katherine Helmond—who we always called Patty, for some reason—played Hannah, and she was sensational. She had been the resident leading lady at the Playhouse since 1961, and she continued there for many seasons. Katherine had a great sense of humor, but she took her work seriously. During the small amount of time that we had free, I often found her sitting on the lawn studying her script. She approached the work in a very professional manner and was a pleasure to work with. Everything was important to her, and she was so specific about all her choices. She's also a very generous performer.

When she and I were on stage, and during the two long scenes she had with Shannon, a defrocked priest working as a Mexican tour guide, apprentices would gather in the wings, watching every moment. I think she inspired many young, budding actors with those performances. She met actor David Christian (now a well-known sculptor) at the Playhouse, and she eventually married him; they've been together ever since. Hollywood soon discovered her, and she created many fabulous television characters. She's probably best known for her role of Jessica on *Soap,* for which she won the Golden Globe Award, and she also played Judith Light's frisky mom on *Who's The Boss?*

David Canary (Adam Chandler of *All My Children* and 'Candy' of *Bonanza)* was just starting out in his career, and he played Hank, the bus driver in this production. (Years later, David and I appeared together again, in the same play, at a theatre in Michigan, and in that production, he played the lead role of Shannon opposite me as Maxine.) Adrian Hall—1964 to 1989 artistic director of Providence, R.I.'s Trinity Repertory Company—was the director, and a Tennessee Williams expert to boot. Lucy Landau, who was featured in the original 1961 Broadway production as Frau Fahrenkopf, was also in our cast. (She had become well known to TV audiences in 1957 when she won $25,000 on the quiz show *Name That Tune.)* And here's some *Dark Shadows* trivia—our one and only Louis Edmonds (Roger Collins) appeared on stage as Algernon with Lucy playing Miss Prism in *Earnest In Love,* a 1960 Off-Broadway musical based on Oscar Wilde's *The Importance of Being Earnest.*

The Night of the Iguana was the first Williams play I appeared in, and it was quite a challenge. He constructed such powerful portraits of the human condition, with such depth, passion, honesty, and lyrical intensity that an actor has to do a lot of "homework" to do justice to one of his characters. Those were the days of a new production every week in summer stock, and each show had just six days of rehearsal. We worked at the Grange (an American-Legion hall) from Tuesday through Saturday, 10 a.m. to 4 p.m. On matinee days, actors who were performing in the current week's production had to stop rehearsing for the new show at 1 p.m. It added up to three-to-six hours of formal rehearsal time each day, and lots of informal times together, discussing our scenes and running the lines. Sunday day was supposed to be our day off, but there was no rest for the weary. Most of us were studying our lines; in the laundry room, at the beach, or just on the back lawn, trying to get letter-perfect. Letter-perfect is perhaps stretching it a bit, but as long as we knew, more or less, what we had to say or do, we were okay. On Sunday evening, we got on stage for the first time for a technical run-through. During a tech, there's no time for acting, just time for a careful working through of the play, with light cues, costume changes, and sound cues. These elements are rehearsed until they work smoothly or until time runs out; remember, there are great time constraints in summer stock.

In this production, however, we still hadn't rehearsed the second act by Friday morning, although our opening was set for Monday! Adrian and all of us in the cast talked so much about the background of the characters, their motivations, and the psychological aspects, that we hardly had time to work on the whole play. It was fascinating, but we were getting nowhere fast, in terms of staging the piece. It could have been panic time, but somehow, miracle of miracles (and that's what summer stock is all about), we pulled it together and got through the tech, and then made it through our dress rehearsal on Monday afternoon, which we did for a small audience of a few friends, apprentices, and resident actors who weren't in the production. In the evening, we had our first performance for a paying audience and it worked; it was actually good. Nonetheless, in stock, it's usually around the fourth or fifth performance that you relax and really start to fly. Then by Saturday night, the eighth performance, you're feeling great, and the show closes!

There's another hitch—if you're in the following week's show, on Tuesday morning of this performing week, you go back to the rehearsal schedule. So, you're rehearsing the new show during the day, and performing the current one at night. It's a mad, whirlwind existence, and we all loved it, and somehow we celebrated many a night at the Cracker Barrel Lounge, and most especially at Maddy's on opening night. Maddy Meredith's Mill Road house was home to most of the resident actors, and her barn was a dorm for the apprentices—and she cooked for all of them. She was a good natured, easygoing woman, who loved the theatre and often played the piano in a production or appeared on the stage in a small part. She turned her house over to the acting company every summer.

There was also the tradition of a champagne party on the theatre's lawn on the first night of the opening play of the season. It was a lovely way for the audience to meet and get to know the cast and crew. The townspeople were extremely supportive of the theatre throughout the season, and I'm certain the party brought them closer to all of us.

After opening in *Iguana,* we began rehearsals for a corny farce of the 1920s, *The Ladies Bump.* It revolves around the reunion of three burlesque queens in the home of one of the ladies who has now become a socialite, played by Katherine Helmond. The second former spear-carrying (bit-player) burlesquer has turned Shakespearean "artiste," and my character, Rose LaMarr, is still doing a few burlesque gigs here and there. The script seemed so inane, and I was concerned that the production could be terrible. But one of the actors who had done the play before told me not to make any judgments, to just throw myself into all the crazy antics, and it would work. He was right. And it succeeded because Alfred directed it; he knew how to get at the heart of the material quickly, without wasting a moment. He had the entire play blocked by the end of the first day, so we had the rest of the week to create and perfect all our comedy *shtick*. Our production was hilarious and the audiences loved it. So did the local critics, as some of their comments reveal:

"*Ladies Bump* is a smash."

"Chuckles, laughter, and downright earthy humor."

"Marie Wallace, as sole active 'shimmy' queen, took down the house with her interpretation of 'The Robert E. Lee' routine." (I think they loved this number because of its seemingly incompatible subjects: The song is all about "waiting on the levy in old Alabamy, waiting for the good ship Robert E. Lee." I was dressed scantily, once more, and held a spear, and shimmied and shook with that come-hither look, and it worked.)

"Fun and boisterous laughter, a riotous farce."

The last play for me that year was *Enter Laughing,* which is about the life of comedian Carl Reiner as a teenage boy, played by Phil Clark. He ends up in a two-bit acting school run by a big-headed, boozing impresario and his daughter (my part), who's on the make for all the young boys. It was a fun way to end the season.

Toward the end of my run that summer, John talked to me about a play called *Burlesque* written by George Manker Watters and Arthur Hopkins. They were planning to do it the following year, and although they hadn't officially asked me to be in it, I took that as a clue that they were interested, and I made a mental note to get a copy of the play and read it as soon as I arrived back in New York. I learned that it had been presented on Broadway in 1927 starring Barbara Stanwyck as Bonny and in 1946 with Bert Lahr as the star, playing Skid. In 1947, it was loosely adapted into a film, *Mother Wore Tights* with Betty Grable and Dan Dailey. Well, just as I hoped, I got a call in the spring of the following year (1965) with an offer to play Bonny in *Burlesque,* along with parts in *Period of Adjustment* and *Ladies Night in a Turkish Bath.*

The company that next year was outstanding, with Ian Sullivan, Richard Kennedy, Dick Sabol, Louis Beachner, Lucy Landau, Denny Drew, and Rue McClanahan. Rue, who went on to great fame with TV's *Maude* and *The Golden Girls,* was a resident actress that year and the next. We had a great time working together.

Burlesque is about a traveling burlesque troupe with most of the scenes taking place in the basement dressing room of a theatre. In the Hampton version, Alfred very cleverly rearranged it so that every time one or two of the performers ran out of the room saying, "There's my cue," the curtain came down, the set moved back, and those same actors ran back onstage doing a song and dance number. Rue was outstanding as Maizie, and in one scene, dressed in strategically placed fig leaves, she did a hilarious version of "Take a Bite of My Apple" (Sample lyrics: "Come take a bite of my apple, so rosy and red, and I'll appease your hunger, Adam and Eve didn't get anywhere, 'til one apple made them a pair"*). The combination of the lyrics, drum rolls, and a few little bumps and grinds made it hysterical.

I'm not a singer, but I sang and danced throughout the show and brought it off successfully. In fact, early on the morning after we opened, I was awakened by a knock on my door. When I opened it, I saw John with newspapers under his arm. He said that we got great reviews. However, he looked terribly concerned. And I said "But???" and John's response was that one of the critics felt there wasn't enough of me (he was referring to the amount of musical numbers I had, not my body). John wanted to know if I'd work with them on an additional number and put it in that night. I had been looking forward to a long sleep-in that morning, since I didn't have a rehearsal call, and there had been a wild opening night party; but this was a great challenge, and I took it.

We decided on "I Can't Give You Anything But Love, Baby." It was a song I had heard many times and knew pretty well. The pianist, John Clifton, found a comfortable key for me and we worked on that for what seemed like only a few seconds! Then we had to dream up a costume. We climbed the long, straight ladder to the costume attic and started digging around. It was steamy-hot up there, so we tore through the place and quickly found many long chiffon scarves and made a quick decision. There would be no sewing involved; I would tuck the strips of chiffon in and around a lacy bikini, and slowly pull each scarf off as the song progressed. This was summer stock and not burlesque, and so even in a play about a burlesque troupe in the 1920s, we didn't strip down to bare bodies. It was all for laughs and the last part of our costume was usually a bikini or fancy underwear. The costume lent itself to a little wild choreography; no set steps, no shoes, just complete abandonment in reaction to the drum riffs and licks, with lots of body movements and tossing of the head with my long hair flying everywhere. It turned out to be a funny number and one of the highlights of the show.

Burlesque was so well received that management decided to play it for another week. I have a great poster from the show with *HELD OVER!!!* pasted across the top, and with parting messages inscribed to me from the cast. Rue's note is especially charming. Using the colloquialisms of the time period of the play, she wrote, "Geez Bonn, Someone as sweet as you has no business being so damned lovely. It's been a treat playing with you, you bird, you darb, you kid, you. Maizie Rue McClanahan."

I worked on one serious play that year, Williams' *Period of Adjustment*, and then another simply-for-laughs-play, *Ladies Night in a Turkish Bath*, their third production of this play. *Ladies Night* was a wild French farce that Hampton audiences adored, and it was one of the theatre's most requested shows. I was a stripper once more (getting typecast?), and Alfred and I worked out a truly hilarious number with me dressed in dozens of balloons. It took place in a women's Turkish bath where a bunch of men, dressed as women, are trapped. Again, the Hampton critics reacted very positively to our high jinks:

"A wild combination of corny jokes, hammy acting, impossible situations, and fantastic gimmicks that will provide you with one of your funniest evenings of the summer."

"Marie Wallace displays a real stack of feminine charms in her unusual second act strip [in] which, instead of hiding behind a single balloon like the famous Sally Rand of by-gone days, Miss Wallace is covered with a dozen balloons and she does her strip act by the simple expedient of a pin that bursts the balloons one at a time."

"A wild night of fun and laughter."

One of the appealing aspects of a theatrical career is the sense of camaraderie between you and your fellow actors, most especially in long-term situations (as a regular on a soap opera, in a long Broadway run, or during a season in summer stock). The Hampton Playhouse was the best example of this. It was a true family, starting with Alfred's mother, Sarah Christie Pine. In fact, on that above-mentioned cherished poster, she signed, "With all my love to my adopted daughter." She was the chief cook and bottle washer, who shopped, cleaned, ran the box office, collected tickets and money at performance time, and even appeared on stage in character roles. One summer I ate at the Big House (that was usually reserved for the management and staff, rather than actors) and it was so wonderful to have family dinner every night. The only problem was that Sarah wanted to keep feeding me, and since her food was so good, I had to constantly remind myself that I'd be going on stage within an hour or so, and I'd better not be too indulgent. It's best to act on a stomach that's only slightly satisfied, certainly not full, since that can be disastrous (falling asleep on stage being the worst, and yes, I once worked with a famous actor who did just that—but in his case it was from too much alcohol, not food).

I always loved to talk to John's mom and dad. I'm sorry I wasn't studying Italian at that time; I might be speaking fluently by now, instead of stumbling through a few phrases. John's father made the best red wine, and occasionally I'd share a single glass with him. On one lazy, warm, non-rehearsal day, we got carried away and I had a second glass, and I found out it was mighty powerful stuff. Luckily, I had a full afternoon to sleep it off, and then I had a great dinner at Sarah's and was ready for the evening performance.

I skipped a summer because I was in the Broadway production of *Sweet Charity,* but right after *Charity* closed, in 1967, I was invited to the Playhouse once again. That was a summer of farce for me—*In One Bed and Out the Other,* and *Strip for Action.* The Playhouse did dramas, comedies, and musicals, and in case you haven't caught on yet, its audiences also liked the risqué French farce. So when John and Al decided to produce *Boeing, Boeing* (a racy comedy, though the title doesn't suggest that), they thought a change in name would attract a bigger audience, so it became *Strip for Action.* It was a more provocative title and still was descriptive of the play (not that we were stripping, but airports do have strips and the play was full of action). They had a talent for changing names; *Ladies Bump* was originally *Stepping Sisters,* not nearly as titillating.

There's another *Dark Shadows* trivia connection here: In *Boeing,* I played Janet, the American Airlines stewardess, and in the 1965 Broadway production, that character was portrayed by Diana Millay (*DS's* Laura Collins). And this is an interesting note—the play lasted only three weeks on Broadway (perhaps it wasn't sophisticated enough for NYC audiences), yet it played in London for three years, five years in Paris, has been a popular standard in theatres around this country for decades, and Paramount Pictures made it into a popular 1965 film starring Tony Curtis and Jerry Lewis.

The plot revolves around an American newspaper correspondent who juggles romances with three flight attendants from Lufthansa, Air France, and American Airlines. All three live in his apartment near Orly Airport in Paris whenever they're in town, which is always at different times. It all works successfully until there's a screw-up in the flight schedules, and lo and behold, all three women end up in Paris (and his apartment) at the same time. One gal walks in the front door as the other one exits to the bedroom, and as the first one closes the bathroom door, the third comes in from another room. As in most farces, it entertained with unlikely yet possible situations, sexual innuendo, a fast-paced plot and numerous doors. In our production, Blythe Danner played the German gal and was very charming. A few years later, in 1969, she won the *Theatre World Award* for her part in The Repertory Theatre of Lincoln Center's production of *The Miser.* In the same year, she landed the lead role on Broadway in *Butterflies are Free,* and her career was launched.

The theatre arranged to get uniforms from Lufthansa and Air France, and American Airlines promised an outfit too, but by Saturday, it hadn't yet arrived. It was decided that Annette (John's niece and a very conscientious worker) would make my costume from scratch. I wasn't worried. We did the tech on Sunday night without it, and I was promised that I'd have it for the dress rehearsal on Monday afternoon. After the tech, I went in to the Big House, and Annette was on the floor just starting to cut out the pattern for my costume. I didn't panic—until Sylvia Miles (featured as the prostitute Cass in the film *Midnight Cowboy* the following year) arrived with her former husband, Ted Brown. They had just driven up from New York, and she would be starting rehearsals in two days for *The Owl and the Pussycat*. She needed a fur coat as part of her costume, and she wanted to be driven around in the morning to shop for one (Ted had to leave very early). She was so convincing in her pleas of urgency that someone suggested that Annette do the chauffeuring. That's when I laid down the law. I said, "Waaaaitttt a minute! My costume is on the floor in fourteen pieces, and my play is opening in less than twenty-one hours. Annette's not going nowhere!" I prevailed and my uniform was delivered to me at 1:30 p.m., just before the dress rehearsal started. Sylvia got her coat early in the week, and she wasn't too upset that everything wasn't dropped for her. In fact, she must not have been too mad, because after she returned to New York, she called me and joined my Central Park jogging group.

During the sixties, when I kept returning to Hampton, I was also working on Broadway (see upcoming chapters for details). But Hampton was such an out-of-the-ordinary experience that I couldn't resist going a bit out of sequence, and putting it all together. I have, however, saved my very special return engagement in the eighties for a later chapter.

In terms of those early years at the Playhouse, 1968 (which was the Playhouse's twentieth season) was another wonderful one: I performed in *Bachelor's Honeymoon* (another name change, originally *Lullaby*; not nearly as attention-grabbing), Neil Simon's *The Star-Spangled Girl,* and Frank Gilroy's *The Only Game in Town.*

Bachelor's Honeymoon, a bittersweet comedy, addresses the age-old problem of newlyweds adjusting to the groom's mother. Comedian Nina Varela played the domineering mother, and Tom Foral played my new husband Johnny. All the laughs come from the living arrangement when the overpowering mother moves in with a neighbor across the hall and tries to win her son back. The women take over this play and the fun is in the battle. Guess who wins?

The Star-Spangled Girl was a "feast of hilarity" according to Hampton critic Ned Brown, and I enjoyed every minute of it. I played Sophie Rauschmeyer, a patriotic, all-American Olympic swimmer, engaged to a Marine. But Sophie's life changes all around when she meets her next-door neighbors, a pair of sixties radicals: one, the impulsive, zany writer Norman played by Reno Roop, the other his writing partner, Andy (Tom Foral). They've spent the past three years and all their money publishing a protest magazine called *Fallout*. Sophie just has a passion for the Red, White and Blue and hates everything their magazine represents but soon finds she's fallen in love with Andy. It's all very lighthearted with extremely funny dialogue and fast-paced action. Once again, it was a real crowd-pleaser.

In *Only Game,* I used an acting trick I picked up somewhere along the way, which is my ability to hide from the audience the fact that I don't know a line. I don't over-react; I stay cool and collected and stare down my opponent (oops, I mean scene partner), never getting that blank, terrified look in my eyes. This can put the other actor at a great disadvantage, since it seems like it's his fault; that *he* went up in his lines. I don't deliberately do it, it just happens. Well, one night when I was on stage in a scene with John, he said his lines to me while I sat at my sewing machine, as directed. I went totally blank; I don't know why that happens, possibly a distraction, a loss of concentration, but there it was. I looked at him for a long moment, and I uttered, "No comment." I then turned away and went back to my sewing. I thought that would give me a few seconds to get back into the scene; that he'd say his line again, and I'd pick up from there. Well, he repeated his line and I was blanker than ever; I couldn't have remembered my own name if I tried. Once again, I stared him down and imperiously stated, "As I said before, NO COMMENT!!!" I then went furiously back to moving that machine needle one hundred miles per hour.

By then, I was about to break up, but I stayed in character and after a few seconds, pushed my chair back, strode past him and across the stage to the wings, where the stage manager sat with the book. As soon as I got off stage, I frantically whispered, "What's my line?" He gave it to me. I stormed back, then turned to John and delivered the line and we went on from there. No one in the audience knew there had been a mistake, except for Alfred (the director). I thought John would be furious with me about it, but instead we laughed over it after the show, and we've had a few good laughs over the years, retelling the story.

I made wonderful friends at the Playhouse, including Al and John, who, besides running a successful summer theatre, gave fabulous parties during the winter. Those were wonderful reunions. You never knew who you'd run into...Ian Sullivan, David Doyle, Bobby Stockbridge, Norman Doucett, Tony LoBianca, Frank O'Brien, Tina Louise, Frank Vohs, Harold Clurman...the list goes on and on. I was lucky enough to return to the Playhouse many years later for an entire summer and work with another favorite actor, Larry Storch. I'll tell you all about that later.

The "boys" ran the Hampton Playhouse for fifty years and influenced so many young actors (probably old ones, too). What joy it was to be there and share the stage with all the hundreds of actors they cast in their shows, and whose lives they touched and changed.

The Right Honourable Gentleman:
Back To My British Accent

A theatre audition, a callback and the call from your agent that you got the part, and the first day of rehearsals often happen quickly. It seems like forever when you're waiting for that call, but the reality is that you can be unemployed one day, with no prospects ahead (or so it seems), and the next day, you're flying high and in a new show. With that formula in mind, the summer of 1965 was an unusual one for me because I auditioned for a new play in June, had the callback right away and won the role, but rehearsals were not to begin until *after Labor Day!* They cast the show well in advance because the director had a busy summer in London and wouldn't arrive back in the States until the first of September.

What a super summer that was. Knowing I was signed for a Broadway play in September, I could relax and have a wonderful time. Greg and I joined a beach club, where I spent hours walking along the shore, usually covered from head to toe to shield my light, freckled, Irish skin. I was also fortunate enough to be in a few shows at the Hampton Playhouse, and they were so enjoyable that it was more vacation than work. It was like being on summer break during my school days, but I must say that I looked forward to that autumn a lot more than I did when I was a kid.

The play was *The Right Honourable Gentleman* by Michael Dyne, a London hit that was in its second year in the West End. Britain's Frith Banbury directed it, for the producing team of Peter Colson, Amy Lynn, and Walter Schwimmer. Rehearsals began on a Tuesday early in September, and we had the great luxury of rehearsing at the theatre in which we were to open. Usually, a show rehearses in a studio until the final days, when the technical rehearsals begin. It's at that point that the actors finally get onto the actual stage. Then there are so many physical adjustments to be made, in a very short period of time, that it can be incredibly stressful. But with this show, we were off to a great start since we were in our theatre from the beginning. It was the Billy Rose Theatre on West 41st Street, named for the Broadway showman best known for composing "Me and My Shadow" in 1959. It's now called the Nederlander Theatre.

I met most of the cast for the first time that day, except for Nancy Reardon. She, Joel Crothers (another future *Dark Shadows* actor), and I had done a show-case production of *Warm Peninsula* earlier in the year, and I was delighted to see her again. We formed a tight bond immediately, along with another actress, Sylvia O'Brien, and those relationships continue to this day. The stars of the show were British: Charles D. Gray, who had recently been on Broadway in *Poor Bitos* and *Kean*; Sarah Badel, daughter of actor Alan Badel, making her U.S. debut; and Coral Browne, who played my mother. Coral was a very stylish Australian actress who worked primarily in Britain, but did some marvelous work in the States on stage and film. (She's best remembered for her portrayal of Vera Charles, Mame's sidekick in the 1958 film *Auntie Mame*. In 1973's film *Theatre of Blood*, her character was electrocuted by Vincent Price, who used a booby-trapped hairdryer. The effect was dynamic, and she must have even found it somewhat romantic; she married him soon after.) The rest of the cast, which included Frances Sternhagen, William Roerick, Henderson Forsythe, M'el Dowd and Staats Cotsworth, were Americans.

The Right Honourable Gentleman is an intriguing drama about a Victorian era Parliament member who was involved in a sex scandal that rocked British politics. He was due for an appointment in the Cabinet, but was disgraced and his career was ruined. After all, it was 1885; today he'd probably become the Prime Minister. The story was especially of interest in 1965 because it paralleled the then-recent (1963) Profumo affair. (John Profumo was a Cabinet minister who had a relationship with showgirl Christine Keeler, which also aroused great outrage...and lots of tabloid coverage.)

The cast had seen the renderings of the costumes on the first day of rehearsals, and mine was to be a beautiful lavender gown, which delighted me. But a few days later, the costume designer, Loudon Sainthill, asked if I would mind switching colors with Coral Browne. Her equally gorgeous gown was to be light green, but she refused to wear that color on stage. It was a superstition I had never heard of before: She felt that it was bad luck to wear green on stage. I learned that there was a fairly common "don't-wear-green" theatre superstition. It started when actors performed outdoors on green grass. If they wore green, they weren't seen very well. Also, in the early twentieth century, a green light (limelight) was frequently used to illuminate the stage, and if an actor wore green under that light, he could appear almost invisible.

I don't have any superstitions and I decided I certainly wasn't going to pick up that one. I especially don't like the superstition about avoiding the term "good luck," and using "break a leg" instead. I like to say what I mean and not beat around the bush. In fact, I know at least one actor (Barnard Hughes during the dress rehearsal of the 1964 Broadway production of *Hamlet*), who took the breaking-legs wishes to heart, and *did* break his leg on stage. So much for good wishes! But back to my costume…I knew that lavender *or* green would be a perfect compliment to my hair and complexion, so I said it was okay. It turned out that the gowns and colors were similarly stunning, and we were both happy. Green didn't bring me any bad luck, either. In fact, during the three-and-a-half week period of rehearsals, my agent Michael called about auditioning for the upcoming musical *Sweet Charity*. Because I was in a serious drama I was very excited about, I wasn't interested in a musical at that point, but it made me feel very confident that there was lots of work out there for me. I did eventually audition for the part of Ursula in *Charity*, but we'll leave that intrigue for the next chapter.

Right Honourable was the first Broadway show I worked on that didn't have out-of-town tryouts. Instead, we did twelve low-priced previews in town, from October 7 to 18, during which we cut and added scenes, changed stage directions, solved technical problems, and generally ironed out any mess we may have gotten into, rehearsing most days, and performing at night and at a few matinees. At that time, many productions started to do in-town previews because it was much less costly than going from city to city. With any luck, a week before the official opening (at which critics were welcome), the show was "frozen" (no more changes). It was an unwritten rule that critics were not allowed to attend and critique a play until it officially opened. That changed somewhere in the seventies and now critics come whenever they please, and many come before opening night.

The New York premiere performance was on October 19. We opened to good reviews, and we were especially pleased when we were referred to as the "all-British cast." (The majority of us were Americans but obviously we'd done such good accents as proper Brits that everyone believed us.) Several critics thought it was old-fashioned drama, but some liked the writing, and I got a big kick out of Whitney Bolton, of the *New York Morning Telegraph*, who wrote, "We have for too long had those lean, pawky, pock-marked tatterdemalions that passed for plays, and now we have one of meat and substance, of stature and importance. What Mr. Dyne has done is to take a rather famed scandalous divorce case of 1885 and retell it in ways that, oddly, have impingement on today." He also went on to say we were "a superior cast, not one of whom is less than perfect in his or her role…all gleam with faultless performances."

The most exciting thing that happened in New York during the run of *Right Honourable* was the Great Blackout on November 9. Everybody who was in the city remembers exactly where he or she was that day and night, and I'm no exception. I was shopping for clothes at my favorite boutique, run by a man named Billy LaReine (he got his name from a cigar wrapper; it was originally Morris Kapner). His shop was on the seventh floor of a building on Broadway, between 52nd and 53rd Streets (right next to the Broadway Theatre, where I had done *Gypsy*).

I had finished shopping and Billy and I were having coffee together, when the lights flickered for a few seconds. Then the lights went out for about six seconds, came up once again, flickered a bit more, and slowly went out completely at 5:27 p.m. At first, we thought it was just happening in the building. But then we looked out the window and saw that the lights in all the other buildings were out too, even the ones across the river in New Jersey. Billy got very concerned, since it was at the height of the Cold War and he thought it was, without a doubt, a Russian invasion. I didn't believe that for a moment; I never felt that our shores could or would be attacked. I'm not an alarmist, so although I had no idea what could be wrong, I wasn't quite so worried. We went out into the hall, as others did, and before long, a workman from the building came along with a flashlight. He told us that people were trapped in the elevators, and that we had to evacuate the building immediately. I left my dresses in Billy's office, and we hightailed it down the stairs and went our separate ways. I was happy to be above ground, since I assumed that subway trains were probably stuck between stops. The streets could have been scary, since it was rush hour and there were no traffic signals; but calm, not panic, overtook the city. Many people went into the middle of the streets and acted like traffic cops, directing the cars through intersections, all politely working together.

My first impulse was to go straight to the theatre, so that I'd be there for the evening show, but I wanted to make sure that Greg was okay, so I headed home. Public transportation wasn't an option and there were no cabs in sight, so I walked. It was a crisp autumn evening, a time of year when it gets dark early in New York, but we had the most beautiful bright night I've ever seen. An extraordinary full moon lit up the sky, and it guided us all home. No one panicked; on the contrary, everyone on the street was cool, cheerful, friendly, and ready to lend a hand. It was a beautiful experience. (The crime rate during the blackout was very low; unlike the 1977 New York blackout, when we had looting and arson and 3,700 people were arrested.) I got home and found Greg was already there, safe and sound. He tried to convince me that there'd be no performance that night, but I still had my "show must go on" attitude and I didn't want to miss it. I tried to get in touch with the stage manager but the phone lines were all out, too. Finally, I settled down, lit a few candles, made a lovely dinner (we cooked by gas), opened a bottle of wine, and enjoyed the evening.

Lights came on slowly the next morning, throughout the day, and into the next day. We did have a performance the next night, although we didn't have full lights, but the Billy Rose Theatre had an emergency generator, so our stage was adequately lit. (Even with the generator, however, we couldn't have played on the night of the blackout since all New Yorkers were incommunicado. Besides, everyone was so happy to finally be home, no one would have dared venture out for a mere theatrical performance.) But on this next night, we were ready and so was the audience. A photographer from *The New York Times* came to our dressing rooms to take some photographs, so we turned off the lights, pulled out our candles, and proceeded to make up under candlelight (it seemed like the dramatic thing to do). There's a book titled, *The Night the Lights Went Out*, with a photo of actress M'el Dowd and me making up, lit only by candles from beneath, and looking like two witches from *Macbeth*. The blackout experience stayed in my mind for a long time, and I carried a flashlight everywhere for a full year after that.

Thanksgiving and Christmas came and went fairly uneventfully, and then we got a "lovely" New Year's Day present: a transit workers' strike which couldn't have come at a worse time. It was very cold and most of us didn't feel like walking, especially once the show ended at 11 p.m. To the rescue came Greg's big ol' Cadillac. He drove me to and from the theatre and on the way there, picked up a number of the cast members, including Coral. It wasn't a long trip to the theatre, but it was enough time for a few good laughs. I always got a kick out of the way Coral addressed Greg. She prefaced everything with, "Doctor, dear," in her smooth, silvery, dulcet tones. The strike was settled within twelve days, the fares jumped from fifteen cents to twenty cents, and we all went back to our regular routine.

The show foundered during the subway strike; it had never been a huge hit, and it lost its momentum. A few of the Broadway columnists kept giving it publicity, which seemed to help for a while. Syndicated columnist Jack O'Brian wrote "[*The Right Honourable Gentleman*] is a fine, fine play, serious in that it is not a dizzy little comedy, and sheer entertainment in its shock-treatment of a theme written brilliantly, plotted beautifully, acted soundly, and produced properly." It didn't help. We closed on January 22, 1966 after 118 performances.

The Right Honourable Gentleman at the Billy Rose Theatre lasted about as long as a school semester, which I guess was fitting, since, like most kids in school, I met Nancy and Sylvia there; two of my *forever friends*.

Sweet Charity and Gwen Verdon's birthday party: with Gwen and Jim Luisi

Sweet Charity

Employed/unemployed, engaged/unengaged, making money/collecting unemployment insurance—that's the back-and-forth nature of this business, and at the beginning of 1966, I was proceeding as could be expected. Another of my Broadway shows closed but, luckily for me, my agent didn't waste any time getting me another job. I started auditioning once again, and one morning, less than three weeks later, I got a surprise call about an audition for *Sweet Charity*. It was a surprise because the show had opened only two weeks before, and I couldn't imagine that there would be a need for a replacement so soon. However, the actress playing *Ursula* (Sharon Ritchie, Miss America 1956 from Colorado) had given her notice, and Michael was right on the ball asking if I wanted to audition for the part. Of course, my answer was, "Yes, indeed!" So, I got the script, studied it, and did a preliminary audition for the production stage manager.

The next day my agent told me that the producers were very interested, and the next step would be to audition for director Bob Fosse. He was out of town on another assignment and wouldn't be in New York for another week or two, so a definite audition date wasn't set. During that time, I had also auditioned for the part of Katherine in the American Place Theatre's production of Ronald Ribman's *The Journey of the Fifth Horse* (based on a short story by Russian playwright Ivan Turgenev), with Dustin Hoffman playing the lead role. As luck would have it, I got the part in *Journey* before the second audition for *Charity* was arranged. Well, I figured a bird in hand was worth holding onto, so I accepted the Off-Broadway play. I make the decision sound easy, but it's always agonizing. If you turn an offer down, and the part in the show you were waiting for doesn't materialize, you have nothing. If you accept the first offer, and then get the desired part, you're faced with walking out of a show and possibly antagonizing the producers and director (who you might want to work with again some day). It can be a real mess. Everyone always consoles you by saying how lucky you are to have two job offers, but I hate going through it.

We started rehearsals of *Journey* on February 21, and as you might have guessed, I got a call the next day that a final audition had been arranged for me at the Palace Theatre prior to the Wednesday matinee. I went to the *Journey*

rehearsal the next morning and on the lunch break, sped over to the Palace Theatre, met and auditioned for Bob Fosse, and got the part! Somehow *Charity* was
meant to be in my life. I gave my closing notice to *Journey*, and was replaced by
Charlotte Rae. (I know we're extremely different types, but it was a real character
part; a big stretch for me. I had gone to the audition with my hair in a little ball
on top of my head, and wearing an old lady dress and character shoes. It would've
been fun to play, but *Charity* was more exciting.) The new contract was drawn up
on February 23, and I did my first performance on March 11.

Sweet Charity is based on Federico Fellini's 1957 film *Nights of Cabiria*, which
starred his wife, Giulietta Masina. It's a brilliant movie about Cabiria, a prostitute
with the proverbial heart of gold. Our American musical version was softened up
a bit. Cabiria becomes Charity Hope Valentine (Gwen Verdon), a dance hall girl,
still with that heart of gold, who works at the Fandango Ballroom in New York
City. The show was conceived, staged, and choreographed by Fosse. (He was
married to Gwen at this time, but their careers were linked together throughout
their lives, both before and after the marriage, from their first meeting in the
Broadway production of George Abbott's *Damn Yankees*, in 1955, when Fosse
was an up-and-coming choreographer.) *Sweet Charity* has a Neil Simon book
with music by Cy Coleman, and lyrics by Dorothy Fields. My character was Hollywood starlet Ursula, who is having a love affair with Italian movie star Vittorio
Vidal (Jim Luisi played and sang the part very flamboyantly).

My opening night for *Charity* was different from any I had done before
because the show had rehearsed for four weeks, played out-of-town, did ten previews in New York and had been running for five additional weeks without me,
so all the other actors were very comfortable in their roles. I had never been nervous before a performance, even on opening nights (some actors suffer from par-
alyzing stage fright). There is definitely a physical change in me as I prepare to go
on stage, but I feel it as heightened excitement, more energy, very upbeat, being
more alive than ever. However, the night I went in to *Charity* was different. The
reason was this: As a replacement you usually rehearse in a studio, with the stage
manager and the understudies, rather than the actors who are currently playing
those parts. Then, a day or two before you open in the part, you have a rehearsal
with the actual cast members. In this situation, I didn't meet Gwen Verdon until
the night of my first performance. We ran through our scene once at "half hour."
(It's a union rule that actors must be signed in and in their dressing rooms a half-
hour before curtain time, although most actors report in much earlier and are
dressed and ready to go at that point.) Gwen said the scene would be fine, wished

me luck, and that was it. I felt okay about it all and went back to my dressing room for some last-minute makeup touches.

I made my entrance for the first scene, outside the nightclub, and all of a sudden I felt the vastness of the Palace Theatre. I had never worked in such a huge theatre. My knees were trembling and I felt like a wind-up doll on "very fast." For a moment, I could hardly concentrate, but I got myself back on track. That's why it's so important to stay focused. (The only other time I quaked like that was in Los Angeles when I went out with my friend Barbara London and tried to ride a horse without any prior instructions—my first and only time on a horse.) My knees calmed down on my second entrance, and the next big surprise came when I flung myself down on the bed for Vittorio. We had been rehearsing using folding chairs to represent the bed, but I assumed that the stage bed would be closer to the real thing. Wrong! It was as hard as a rock and that threw me for a moment, especially since it hurt. After that first night, I learned how to make it look like I was throwing myself down as I lay down very gently in reality. It's all an act up there anyway, so it's best not to get too realistic.

In that opening scene, Vittorio and Ursula are in the midst of a big lover's quarrel. Charity watches the whole scene in awe. As Ursula storms off, vowing never to see him again, Charity just happens to bump into him. She feels sorry for him and tries to offer comfort, and he immediately invites her to his apartment. She's so thrilled to be with a movie star and asks him for a memento so that her friends will believe she was there. When he goes off stage to get her the first item, she slowly starts singing and dancing. He gives her more and more of his things: a photograph, a cane, a top hat, and she is soon into her show-stopping number, "If My Friends Could See Me Now." Unfortunately for Charity, Ursula arrives back at the apartment to beg Vittorio's forgiveness. Before he lets Ursula in, he hides Charity in a closet. (In there, Gwen was eating a hot dog, drinking a beer, and *smoking*, all of which the audience saw because the fourth wall to the closet wasn't there.)

The juxtaposition of the two elegantly clothed actors ranting and raving, and the little waif inside the closet created a hilarious scene. It was especially comical when Gwen propped her head against the door to listen more intently, and I pounded on it wailing, "Vittorio, Vittorio, Vittorio," with each thumping getting harder and harder. I wish I could've seen her reaction, but I know from the nonstop laughter at every performance, and from photos of the scene, that she was reacting like mad, with both her face and body. Jim (Vittorio) then sang a love song to me, and we eventually moved off to the bedroom, leaving Charity alone with her memories.

I had always admired Gwen Verdon before I had the opportunity to work with her. (Who could forget her as Lola and her sleek and sinuous rendition of "Whatever Lola Wants" in the film version of *Damn Yankees*?) When I shared the stage with her, I discovered that she was an extraordinary person too: gracious, caring, and lots of fun. She set the tone for the show, and it spread throughout the cast. The rest of the cast was top-notch too, with John McMartin as Oscar, Charity's nervous boyfriend; Helen Gallagher as Nickie and Thelma Oliver as Helene, Charity's sidekicks; Ruth Buzzi as The Good Fairy; Arnold Soboloff as Daddy Johann Sebastian Brubeck; and all the sensational singers and dancers. It was a great group.

In the story, everyone takes advantage of Charity, and she usually gets the wrong end of the stick. Nevertheless, in the end Charity triumphs because she believes in the goodness of people, and always has hope—most especially when Ruth Buzzi (actress/singer/comedienne extraordinaire) came dancing out dressed as the Good Fairy singing, "Tonight, Tonight, Dreams will come true tonight." It's near the end of the play and Charity has had her purse stolen by a new boyfriend, who had promised marriage but instead pushed her into the Central Park Lake (the orchestra pit). She sees the lovely fairy as she's climbing out of the lake, and her faith is restored. She turns toward the audience knowing life is good, as the fairy turns her back to us, and we see she's wearing a sandwich card advertising The Good Fairy *Restaurant*. It's a very funny scene, indeed.

I wore a beautiful, white sleeveless fur coat and two different dresses in the show. One was a long sheath gown with lots of pearls and beads, and it looked fabulous. The other costume was a knee-length white silk dress. The material in the second dress was beautiful, and draped very nicely, but the style was plain. It had a scoop neck, neither low nor high, cap sleeves, and a gathered skirt. I was playing a very glamorous lady, and the dress looked okay, but I was glad when it started to wear out, and the producers said they'd like to replace it. I went to a number of stores with the stage manager, but we couldn't find anything that met my approval. That night, back at the theatre, Gwen asked me if I found a dress, and I told her that nothing was suitable. She said, "You make such wonderful clothes, why don't *you* make the costume? We'll get the materials, and the wardrobe mistress will help you, and we'll even pay you to do it." The show was produced by Fryer, Carr & Harris but Gwen was a major stockholder so she could make those decisions. She knew that Ruth Buzzi and I had sewing machines, and that we made many of our clothes at that time, often showing them to Gwen, and she always liked them. Well, I thought it would be great fun to make a costume, and I said I'd do it just for the love of it, but I didn't want to be paid for it.

However, they insisted on paying me and I must admit they got their money's worth. I made a *great* dress. The new one was perfect for a movie queen wannabe: two layers of material, off-white lace over silk, cut on the bias. It was a basic Simplicity pattern but I embellished it. The dress had a V-neck, spaghetti straps, and was very sexy. What I liked most about it (besides wearing it) is that when the show was produced in London, they copied my version of the dress!

When one of our stage managers, Michael Sinclair, made a Noah's Ark as a birthday present for Gwen and Bob Fosse's daughter, Nicole, he also brought in patterns of all the animals from the Ark. Someone decided that the cast would make all those little cloth animals (two each), and Ruth and I thought that was a terrific idea. We got started on them and they looked adorable. No one else seemed to want to do theirs, so we ended up making *all* those little guys. I began to wonder if I was cast for my sewing abilities or my acting. It was tedious, but also fun and very gratifying to see Nicole's reaction to the Ark and to all the animals.

During the run, Gwen had a birthday coming up (January 13), and we wanted to do something special for her party. We decided we'd all create unique costumes and put on a silly show, which we would do right after our performance that night. Most of us hung out at a restaurant called Gus & Andy's, which was right next door to the Palace's backstage entrance on 47th Street, and that's where we had the party. Jim Luisi acted as the M.C., and I don't remember what anyone else did, except for Buzzi and me. She and Buddy Vest dressed up as Viking warriors and sang opera (it was hilarious, and she'd made the costumes, of course). I found a song about a girl from Shamokin P-A and other far-off places." The tale goes that her mother taught her ballet ("pointe, plié, pointe, plié, second to left and relivée") but she "gave it up, it didn't pay." So she ends up as a burlesque dancer—all my Hampton experiences had taught me a thing or two. I made the costume (once again) and, if I must say so myself, it was a riot. I wore a full white leotard, with huge red hearts covering my torso, and on top of my head, a small heart on a spring that bobbed up and down constantly. The hearts were very fitting for a *Sweet Charity* party, since that was the logo used on the show's poster. The hearts came off to reveal a bikini outfit, the top of which I fashioned after the first costume I wore on Broadway in *Gypsy* (two huge Christmas balls). When I came running down the stairs in that restaurant, singing that song and doing my pointe, pliés, and then the bumps and grinds, Gwen literally fell to the floor, laughing. We all had a great time that night.

Gwen was an extremely generous person, both in mind and spirit. She really got to know everyone in the cast, and in the crew as well. She was very much like

Robert Preston in that respect. She was a joy to be around. Fosse was fun too, although we didn't see him as much, and since I'd missed that bonding time of rehearsals and out-of-town tryouts, I didn't really get to know him well. However, I have a lovely memento from Gwen and Bobby that they gave us at Christmas: a Tiffany silver plate that sits on my cocktail table to this day. They gave several parties for us through our run, the most memorable being for our one-year anniversary, where we all danced 'til four in the morning. Another unforgettable time was an all-day picnic at a Long Island house they rented for the summer. There was a huge pool and throughout the afternoon and well into the night, we swam, drank, ate, danced, and had a ball.

As you know by now, in almost every show I've been in, I've formed a friendship with one or more of the actors, and we've remained good friends forever. In *Charity*, my favorite actor was Ruth Buzzi. Buzzi (that's what we always called her) and I hit it off right away. Her dressing room was adjacent to mine, and the timing of our parts seemed to coincide, so we had lots of wonderful conversations and laughs, and of course, our sewing sessions. We were very compatible, except for one thing. I love air-conditioning, the colder the better; she likes it cool…to a point. There was one air-conditioner that filtered into both our dressing rooms. I wasn't aware of that, and I just automatically turned it on every night (the controls were in my room). I kept that up until I went into her room one night to find her sitting at her sewing machine with her coat and hat on. She even had the vent closed up with cardboard, but that cold arctic air was coming in, in spite of it. After that, I became more considerate about the room temperature.

Another interesting friendship was formed when, many years after the show closed, I ran into *Charity* dancer Bick Goss (by then a busy director). We hadn't gotten to know each other well during the show, but on that one afternoon on the streets of New York, we caught up on each other's lives, and we picked up our friendship from there.

Like all good things, the production came to an end on July 15, 1967. It was a wonderful year-and-a-half for all of us, both on and off stage of the Palace Theatre during the 608 performances of *Sweet Charity*. Since I've never owned a crystal ball, I was uncertain about what Life or the Theatre would have in store for me after that. Little did I know that my next significant job would have a dark shadow over it.

PLAYBILL

The Palace Theatre

Sweet Charity

Ruth Buzzi

Dark Shadows:
Marie Wallace with
(clockwise) David Selby,
Grayson Hall,
Nancy Barrett,
and Jonathan Frid

Dark Shadows

After *Sweet Charity* closed, Greg and I took an extended trip to Florida for some R&R. Once we had enough of the hot weather, we came back and I got involved with theatre workshops and went to acting class for a while. It's a good idea to occasionally take a refresher course to get back to basics. Actors learn a great deal in the actual work situation, on stage, with an audience, but sometimes we pick up a few bad habits, too. A good class helps to get rid of the superfluous. I also studied with David Craig (husband of comedienne Nancy Walker) at a workshop that was geared toward actors who were auditioning for musicals. Most of us were principally actors, not singers, but we knew that there'd come a day when we'd have to learn a song or two, work with an accompanist, and perhaps even sing at an audition. David taught us how to use all our acting techniques in presenting the story within the song. I'd had some experience at the Hampton Playhouse, but I knew I would benefit from this training. Besides, it was the most popular class in New York. The classes were interesting and attracted the best actors in New York. My classmates were Anthony Perkins, Eileen Heckert, my friends Salem Ludwig and Eulalie Nobel, and a slew of others, less known, but equally talented. I also filmed a number of commercials in that time period. Among them were Miller Lite with Sheldon Leonard, when I played his gun-moll, and Orange Plus, where I played a nineteenth century serving wench and threw a live chicken out the window.

Then, along came the summer of '68, and I was up at the Hampton Playhouse doing several shows. As was our usual routine, during the run, I spoke to Greg every night by phone, after the show. One night he told me that agent Jeff Hunter had called earlier in the day to ask if he could submit me for a role in the ABC/TV show *Dark Shadows*. Neither of us knew much about the show, except that it was a popular afternoon TV series and had a vampire as its star. Since Greg knew what my answer would be, he just said yes for me. Jeff wasn't my official agent at that point. I had met him informally on Seventh Avenue while I was reminiscing with Charlotte Rae (his client) about *The Beauty Part*. We had a nice, quick conversation; he complimented me on the various roles he had seen me in, and he was on his way. When this role came up, my name and image just popped into his head. (He probably didn't represent an actress quite like me, and he thought I was just right for the part.) I returned to New York a few weeks later and called him to set up the audition.

On his first approach to the casting director, Linda Otto, he was turned down because she said that, although I was an excellent actress, I simply wasn't right for the part of Eve. (She saw almost every important theatrical production in New York, and had been to many that I'd been in, and I'd never played a part like Eve.) Fortunately, Jeff was a strong agent, and he prevailed and got me the initial interview with her. After auditioning for her, she repeated that I wasn't what creator/producer Dan Curtis had in mind, but she did like my reading and said she'd set up the audition anyway. She added that I shouldn't feel too bad if he had me in and out of his office in a minute because I wasn't the type he was looking for. Wow, I felt like I had two strikes against me, going for the third. Should I stop while I was still ahead? No way—she got my Irish up and I thought, "I'll show her!"

A few days later, I went to the *Dark Shadows* studio, at 433 West 53rd Street, to audition. I spent about fifteen minutes in Dan's office talking to him and reading a scene. He liked my reading and asked me to look over another Eve scene and read that for him. He was gracious, very direct, and didn't waste too much time. I sat in the outer office studying the new scene, and when I was called back in, the show's producer, Robert Costello, and the head writer, Sam Hall, were there, and that reading went well, too. All in all, I spent over an hour in his office, so it wasn't quite what the casting director made me expect. I left feeling very positive and ran to the restaurant for a late lunch with my long-time friend Justine Johnston (we met in *Electra*). My habit was to check in with my telephone answering service before 5 p.m. every day. (Today people use answering machines and cell phones, but I always enjoyed having a real, live operator taking my messages.) Sure enough, they had a message from my agent and from Dan Curtis Productions. I had a callback! It was for a few days later, but first I had to go to the studio to meet with the costume designer, Ramse Mostoller, to be fitted for a gown. I knew that it was probably down to one or two other actresses being considered for the part, because that's the only time they put an actor in costume for an audition. I eagerly arrived at the show's costume department, and while being measured, I discovered that three actresses were being considered for the role of Eve: a blonde, a brunette, and a redhead (the latter, of course, was me). I tried on a few gowns and one was picked and adjusted for my figure. I don't remember the details of the gown or its color—I was too excited to notice.

At 4 p.m. on the day of the audition, right after that day's taping, I arrived at the studio and was assigned a temporary dressing room. I then met Vinnie Loscalzo, makeup artist supreme, who did his magic on me. I nearly always styled my own hair, and I stuck to form that day, although the show's hair stylist, Edith Tilles, an old friend of mine (she was the first professional stylist to lay a hand on my hair during my modeling days), put her touches on it. I then changed into my gown and was ready. Ten minutes later, we were summoned downstairs to the TV studio, and that's when all three actresses got to see each other. The other two women were tall and beautiful, and had very long, straight, silky, down-to-the-waist hair, à la Vampira or Morticia Adams. But Curtis wasn't casting for another vampire; Eve was a woman built by Dr. Julia Hoffman (played by the talented Grayson Hall) out of old bones that Willie Loomis (John Karlen) found in the mausoleum. Who knew what *that* should look like?!

I decided I could look completely different than my competition by playing up my thick, shoulder-length hair. So I went into a corner, took my handy hairbrush, and backcombed my hair, making it wild and sexy. I waited in a corner and watched what the director asked of the first actress in front of the camera. We had no scripts at that point. They had picked all three of us for our acting abilities; now they were strictly going for a look, a persona. They called the actress closest to the camera and had her start. The directions were all physical: "Walk toward the camera, turn away, look back over your shoulder, give a sly sexy glance." I reverted right back to my *Gypsy* audition—I figured I'd watch what the other actresses did and then go one step further. The first actress probably felt a little silly, and the second one seemed more comfortable with it, but since I maneuvered to be third, I knew what Dan Curtis wanted and was totally relaxed. The mental image I kept was that of a stalking lion (I had the mane of hair to pull it off), and I retained that picture until they yelled, "Cut!" I was told later that on my last prance toward the camera, Dan threw up his script and said, "That's it, hire her!" I like to think that's true.

My agent was called; fees were agreed upon; and a few days later, I was back in the studio makeup room with Vinnie, who had to design my scar makeup. Eve was being created as a mate for Adam, a monster produced in the same laboratory, and Adam had lots of scars across his face and neck. You may have gathered by now that the storyline was loosely based on Mary Shelly's *Frankenstein* and Eve was *The Bride of Frankenstein,* although we were called Adam and Eve. Decisions had to be made as to how many and what kind of scars I'd have. The producers knew they didn't want scars on my face, but they did want some around my neck. Vinnie worked his artistry on my throat for at least an hour, and when he finished, a Polaroid was taken. I wore a purple V-neck dress that day, and the lights picked up the purple colors in the scar, and it looked like a beautiful necklace instead of a scar from sewing a head onto my body. After everyone examined both my neck and the photograph, they chose to get rid of the scars. Hooray—one hour less in the makeup chair every day! We could justify a scarless head by the fact that this was the second experiment under the guidance of Dr. Hoffman, and she had perfected her methods.

The following week, on October 3, 1968, I was back at the studio for a pre-rehearsal of Episode 595. This was done for every script and took place on the day before the actual rehearsal and taping. It ran from 4:30 to 6:30 p.m. I met Jonathan Frid, Grayson Hall, Robert Rodan, Thayer David, and Erica Fitz. They played, respectively, Barnabas Collins, Dr. Julia Hoffman, Adam, Professor Stokes and Leona Eltridge. Except for Erica, all of the actors had been on the show for many months and were very comfortable in their parts and at the studio. It was their home, and I was the new kid on the block. I always felt that the first day of walking onto a set with an established cast was like going to meet your boyfriend's entire family on Christmas Eve. It can be uncomfortable, because you feel like such an outsider. But the *Dark Shadows* actors and the director of my first episode, Sean Dhu (known as Jack) Sullivan, put me at ease immediately, introducing themselves and welcoming me. There were snacks and coffee in the room, and Grayson was the first to offer me some. There was light banter back and forth, and since they were doing most of the talking I had a chance to observe them carefully. They had worked all day and just finished taping a show, but they were full of enthusiasm for the next script. They were the most interesting looking actors I'd ever worked with. The most impressive thing about Jonathan was his voice; it was, and is, magnificent. It was not surprising to learn that he had a long career as a Shakespearean actor. His high cheekbones were also very impressive, as were Grayson's. In fact, they both had the highest cheekbones I'd ever seen, and the hollow below their cheekbones was so deep, it added to their most unusual looks. Thayer reminded me immediately of the great film character actor Sydney Greenstreet (*The Maltese Falcon*), although not as fat, but with the same wonderful voice. Robert Rodan was the tallest actor I'd ever worked with, and one of the handsomest. We were off to a good start!

We talked and joked for about fifteen minutes and then we gathered around a table to read. The script, written by Ron Sproat, was timed during that first reading; the actors gave suggestions for changes; cuts and additions were made. We got up on our feet and the director gave us some general blocking (basic moves). We then said goodnight and went home to study our scenes, since the bulk of the work would be done starting at 8 a.m. the following day. Actually I didn't have anything to do or say in that episode, except lie on an operating table and moan at the very end, as I came to life. There was no pressure on me at all. It was a comfortable way to ease myself in to a new show.

The next morning I arrived at the studio at 7:45 a.m. and discovered, to my amazement, a large group of young fans at the stage door. They already knew who I was and the role I was playing! The show had spawned many fan clubs, and their young members stayed well-informed. I talked with them and signed a few autographs before going inside. Once upstairs, I found the dressing room assigned to me, and I went to the rehearsal hall for the juice, coffee, and pastry that was always provided. There were morning greetings and then we got started quite promptly. I learned the schedule that we would always follow: refining the blocking of the entire show in the rehearsal hall; moving down to the studio for on-camera blocking (positioning the actors on the set); director's feedback; a run-through (rehearsing on camera from beginning to end, in street clothes, and making any changes that were needed); additional notes; dress rehearsal; last-minute notes from producers and director; and finally, at 3:15 p.m., the taping (recording on videotape, to be broadcast at a later date). That was our eight-hour day, with small breaks in between for lunch, and makeup and hair touchups.

Loyal *DS* fans know all the storylines backward and forward (certainly better than we actors remember it...) but for those of you who may never have seen an episode (is that possible?), a little background might help explain things. For many weeks before my first live appearance, a bandage-wrapped dummy had been lying on the operating table in the lab totally covered with a sheet, while Dr. Hoffman, Professor Stokes, and Barnabas worked on bringing Eve to life, without success. They had previously achieved their mission with the "birth" of Adam and were now attempting to create a companion for him. I replaced the dummy, but unlike it, under the white sheets, I was dressed in a black diaphanous gown and high-heeled suede shoes, and had gorgeously coifed hair. Bandages were wrapped around my face, just like they had been on the dummy. Dr. Hoffman's experiment was conducted again, using a terminally ill woman named Leona Eltridge as the life force. In an unintended twist, Eve turned out to be the reincarnation of France's eighteenth-century murderess Danielle Roget, who was considered the most evil woman who ever lived. If you're a fan of anagrams, you can see that LEONA ELTRIDGE can be turned into DANIELLE ROGET, and of course Professor Stokes discovered that after Eve came to life.

In my first scene, Dr. Hoffman pulls some levers and colored water moves through tubes. There are lots of concerned looks, and several screams from Leona until she dies. Adam anxiously unwraps the bandages, and he cries out, "Her eyes are open. She is alive! She is alive!" My eyes *were* open, staring up at the huge, bright, hot spotlights, and I was working feverishly not to blink, but I still looked deader than a doornail. There's disappointment on their faces, but Dr. Hoffman examines my vital signs and states that my heartbeat and pulse are normal, and that she wants to measure my brainwaves. Just then I move again and moan a couple of times, and they know it's a success! I'm alive! I got through my first day on a soap without incident, except for my eyes watering a bit, but I'm proud to say that I never blinked.

We were working with "live" tape; that is to say, we taped each episode from beginning to end without stopping, except for the exact few minutes it would take to later insert the commercials. Because editing was time-consuming and expensive, the tape was only stopped in case of an extreme emergency—which meant almost never. Of course this meant that occasionally some technical mistakes made it on the air (along with a few actor errors…) but I believe that made the show even more fun to watch. It was transmitted into fans' homes a week or so later, but as far as the actor was concerned, it was live. That made it very exciting, unlike today's method of stop-and-go, out-of-sequence taping.

I knew that once we started taping, we were to go straight through with only those commercial breaks. What I didn't know was that the rule was written in stone. No way did you stop—*not for any reason.* So in the second week, when the set in which I was working started to collapse and looked like it was going to fall directly on me, I innocently stopped, dropped character, and became Marie. That was the wrong thing to do since they had no choice but to stop tape. I learned then and there that the only time we stopped was when the director yelled, "Stop Tape!" I think the only disaster that brought those words to his mouth was if a dead man walked. Well, live and learn; or in my case, act and learn.

A month after I began working there, we had a Halloween party at the studio. Of course, that was a fitting holiday for this cast to celebrate. Besides the cast, directors, writers, and production staff, a few magazine writers and the casting director, Linda Otto, attended. I was gratified when she congratulated me on my performances and admitted that she had been wrong in her original assessment. I was also happy that she had taken the chance and arranged the audition with Dan Curtis.

Eve was created for Adam but as soon as she wakes up and sees him, she takes an immediate dislike for him, which is putting it mildly, since, a few days later, she tells Nicholas (Humbert Allen Astredo) that she hates Adam and wants to kill him. Adam keeps trying to win her over, but she insists on going after Jeff Clark (Roger Davis). Unknown to Jeff, he is actually a time-traveler with amnesia. In the past, known as Peter, he was in love with Danielle Roget. Eve remembers him as her lover and wants to get close to him once more. He (as modern-day Jeff) has no interest in Eve. After all, he's preparing to marry Victoria Winters (Alexandra Moltke), and the names Peter Bradford and Danielle Roget mean nothing to him. Are you utterly bewildered by now? I could easily have been, but I could always depend on avid *DS* fans to keep these stories straight.

Humbert played a warlock and I had a great time working with him. He was basically Eve's lord and master, and she didn't like that one bit. But it brought a lot of excitement to our scenes, since he's a fabulous actor, and sparks were always flying when we got together.

As I did more episodes, I met and worked with the two other principle directors, Lela Swift and Henry Kaplan. It was rare to have a woman television director; I had never worked with one before, but it was a man's field for a long time. In fact, Lela was a pioneer in the field, the first woman to direct TV shows, starting in the 1950s on the classic drama anthology *Studio One*. It was many years after her entry that other women were accepted, and she certainly opened the door for them. Our directors all had different styles, but were equally interesting, and I learned a great deal about working in front of a camera from them. I was always amazed that they could put our shows together so expertly in a very short period of time. My only regret is that I never got to work with them in other productions.

In Episode 623, Angelique (Lara Parker) hypnotizes me, preparing to send me back to 1795 when Eve lived as Danielle Roget, and where she'd get a chance to see her Peter Bradford. Television magic had me miraculously disappear out of the chair as the scene ended. I then ran across the entire studio to the next set. As soon as I got there, a cape was thrust on me and a wig with a little lace headdress was plopped on my head. There was only time for Edith, the hairstylist, to secure it with two bobby pins before she was shoved out of the scene as the camera came up on me in the new (actually, old) century. In the dress rehearsal, we proceeded as stated above and as the new scene began, I could hear frantic whispers. They were coming from Edith and I was annoyed because I thought she was simply fussing about the wig not being on straight. Even in a dress rehearsal, you didn't stop for things like that. Then all of a sudden, I heard very fast, heavy footsteps coming toward me. The next thing I knew, a stagehand was grabbing the wig off my head, throwing it to the floor, and stomping on it. It was on fire! In the rush, I had been totally oblivious to lit candle sconces on the wall and backed right into them. Dear Edith had been trying to save me (and the wig!) and I got irritated with her. Now, with disaster averted, I thanked her and the stagehand, and we completed the scene. After notes from Lela, we did the actual taping and it went very smoothly, without incident. Of course, she did move me away from the wall and the candles. Since they didn't stop tape for too many things, I'm glad my little fire episode happened in the run-through, or I might have done my scene in flames!

In any event, Eve returns from the past with an important book that predicts the future, and *convinced* that Jeff Clark is Peter Bradford. She continues to stalk Jeff, which gets Adam more and more angry. One of my favorite lines came when I was up in a room with Adam and I was staring out the window at, of course, Jeff. Adam commanded me to get away from the window and I turned to him and imperiously said, "You may tell me where I am to go, but you will *not* tell me where I can look." I said that with a straight face and meant it. In later years, when I saw a rerun of it, it just made me giggle.

Roger Davis was an especially impulsive actor and occasionally surprised his *DS* acting partner with a new piece of business (changing the blocking, or creating new dialogue) during the taping. There were times when that made it more interesting, and the other actor could pick up on it, and the whole scene would become more alive. But sometimes it was startling and could throw the actor. In one scene with him, I was literally thrown out of frame (out of camera range). His character demanded that I get away from him, and throughout the rehearsals he never touched me. But during the taping, he shoved me and I went flying. I had very high heels on so I didn't have solid grounding. That made me mad because it looked bad (and, of course, no one yelled "Stop tape," so we kept going). When the taping was over, I was waiting for him, ready to bite his head off, but he apologized and said it just happened spontaneously, and he couldn't help himself. He was so charming, and so convincing, that I naturally forgave him.

As any good *DS* fan knows, I played Eve until Adam found me in Jeff's room, on a very stormy night, with lots of thunder and lightning—a great setting for my character's spectacular ending. During the fight, I said the meanest things to him, including, "I can't stand the sight of you. You're ugly! Ugly—do you understand that word? Ugly!" Well, that did it. He lost his timidity and we had a fierce struggle, with my hair flying everywhere, and Adam eventually choked Eve to death. That wasn't the complete end, since I had to play dead on a closet floor for a few more shows, working very hard to keep my eyes wide open and not to blink. I can still feel the fear I experienced as I concentrated, eyes tearing, wanting to blink, but willing myself not to. And then I was gone, but I wasn't forgotten.

At that point, I had an active fan club, run by Cathe Horodowitz. Right from the beginning of my appearances at the studio, the fans were wonderful. They hung out by the stage door both before and after the show. Many offered to start a fan club for me, and the lovely teenager that got to me first was chosen. Remember, this was before Internet sites, so information was usually conveyed via fan newsletters—and *Dark Shadows* had millions of ardent followers. It was one of the most highly rated daytime dramas of all time. I answered all my fan mail, sent photos, took some fans out to late lunch after the taping, and even arranged for them to visit the studio once. We were busy with the show so we couldn't spend too much time visiting with fans. I do think, however, that the personal letters and the autographs and photos were what the fans wanted and cherished. The Marie Wallace Fan Club was only active during my two-year period with *Dark Shadows*, but *DS* fandom continues on forever. And I still see some of those same Stage-door Johnnys and Joans (Richie, Marty, Jay, Mary, Rodney), at annual conventions, called *Dark Shadows* Festivals, along with thousands of fans every year. Fans were always an integral part of *DS*, and I'm sure one of the main reasons we're still so popular is because of our fans' enthusiasm.

Once Eve was really dead (again), my agent arranged some auditions for me and, after the first of the New Year of '69, I signed a contract for the play *Goodbye Charlie*, starring Fannie Flagg. It had a silly, but funny, plot written by George Axelrod, about a guy being shot by his jealous wife and coming back to earth as a woman. (The reincarnated Charlie was Fannie, and I played Rusty Mayerling, Charlie's former girlfriend.) Rehearsals for it began on January 28 (my mom's birthday), and a week later we opened at the Club Bene in Morgan, New Jersey. We were scheduled to run for a limited period, which worked out great since *Shadows* was like a repertory company, and by March, I was back at the studio playing a totally new character, not related in any way to Eve. It was Jenny Collins, lovingly referred to as "Crazy Jenny," and living in the year 1897. This time I didn't have to audition (that's why I call it a rep company); if Curtis and the writers and directors liked your work, you never really died.

There was much that went on in Jenny's life before she appeared on the show. (It's what actors call the backstory and is only for the mind of the actor—it gives us insight into the motivations of a character and helps to create truth in that character.) She was married to Quentin (David Selby) and after a short period of time, became pregnant, at which point, Quentin abandoned her for another woman. She didn't adjust to that well, and when she gave birth to the twins, she went crazy, and was locked up in the attic (shades of Charlotte Bronte's *Jane Eyre*). When Jenny appeared on the show, she was totally crazed—out of her mind. And we slowly discover that there was more to Jenny's deep, dark past; she was actually a gypsy and sister to Magda Rakosi, played by Grayson Hall. Somehow Jenny had a relatively refined accent, while Magda spoke with a thick Hungarian accent. Grayson wore tons of makeup to look like a dark-skinned gypsy, whereas I had a soft, pale complexion. That difference in appearance was never explained, but anything can be justified in the world of make-believe. Jenny had been a singer, so I made up the backstory that when she was working in one of the nightclubs, the owner took her under his wing, paid for her vocal training, and taught her proper speech and civil manners. Quentin first saw her at the club, and they fell in love—but their class differences doomed their marriage.

I wanted Jenny to look very different from Eve, so I came up with a really wild hairdo. (Jenny was, as we'd say today, "mentally unbalanced," and the Collins family kept her hidden in a tower room. Therefore, I reasoned that Jenny would "let herself go," and never let anyone near her hair. That's why it hadn't been combed for months—hence the wild hairdo.) I'm sure many viewers thought I was wearing a fright wig but it was actually the work of my handy hairbrush that helped me backcomb and tease my hair to total wildness. The night before the shoot, I also made little pin curls around my face and on the day of the shoot, I just took out the clips and let the curls dangle. Then Vinnie put false lashes on both the top and bottom of my lids creating a truly crazed look.

In place of her twins, Jenny was given two dolls to play mother to, and she was tolerably content up in the attic with her nursemaid, Beth (Terry Crawford), attending to her every need. However, when "Quentin's Theme" (written by Bob Cobert) was played on the Victrola downstairs, Jenny went ballistic, and usually managed to escape. Once she even got a little violent when Roger Davis (playing the character of Dirk Wilkins) brought coffee to her on a huge silver tray. I (as Jenny, of course) petulantly knocked it off the table he had put it on, and as he bent over to clean up the spill, I cleverly picked up that lovely tray and hit him over the head. I wanted *out*. (Notice, as I'm writing, how the third person occasionally turns into the first person, or goes back and forth from character to actor—that's what occurs when an actor gets so involved with his character, and it happens most especially on a soap.)

Jenny, unlike Eve, had so many levels, and I could really explore my psyche with her. In fact, once I took a walk during a lunch break—unusual for me because I preferred to stay in my dressing room, or around the studio (in my cocoon), but it was a beautiful day and I just wanted to get some air. I like to stay in character (in my head) through the day, especially for a TV show, and apparently a couple of friends riding past in a cab saw me as I was wandering down Tenth Avenue. One of them, writer Sunny Rogers, called me the next day, and said, "Marie, I saw you out walking yesterday and you looked like you'd gone off the deep end. What's happened?" I suppose I sounded pretty sane on the phone, and she finally believed I was simply an actress preparing for her role.

One escape Jenny made was fatal for her. She was searching for Quentin and found him, but unfortunately he was busy seducing Beth, and that infuriated Jenny. As Quentin and Beth were kissing passionately, Jenny snuck up and raised her knife, and as she was about to plunge it into Quentin's back, Beth screamed. Quentin and Jenny had a big wrestling match, but he got the best of her and strangled her to death. That was the end of my second character on the show, except for a few appearances as Jenny's ghost. I went off and got involved in theatre, including my favorite summer theatre, the Hampton Playhouse.

As was consistent with *DS*, after a few months, I got a call to play yet another character—Megan Todd. I was once more delighted to go back to my "repertory company" at the 53rd Street studio. Megan was the owner of the local antique shop, married to Philip Todd, played by Chris Bernau. Fans know this storyline as "The Leviathan Period," and there were all kinds of mysterious happenings during that time, and I was to be part of that, too. At one point, a baby boy named Michael was born to Megan (quite miraculously, since she was never pregnant). And did that baby grow up fast! These days on soap operas, often a young character will be aged quickly, so that he becomes an interesting character. He/ she will go off to boarding school as a ten-year-old and come back a few months later as a twenty-year-old. But in this *DS* storyline, it was intentional—he was a supernatural creature, and he naturally aged to adulthood very quickly.

Four actors played the part at varying stages (three actually, since the newborn was a doll). And that baby grew up to be Jeb Hawkes, played by Chris Pennock, who was much taller than I and about my age. To get an in-depth understanding of any of these plots, it's best to find the *DS* tapes or DVDs and view them for yourselves. If it's your first time watching the show, it'll be a real treat for you. Or ask an ardent *DS* fan—he'll know all the stories and have most of the answers. Fans remember it more clearly than we do!

As grim as things were at Collinwood, it was an even sadder period in my real life. Dear Greg had a heart attack while I was playing Megan, and it became a very intense time. On the days I taped, I couldn't visit him until after the show. As soon as I could get out of the studio, I'd hop in a cab and race over to the hospital on the other side of town and spend the rest of the evening with him. They kept him in the Intensive Care Unit for a long time. I think they were bending over backward to care for him because he was a doctor. Sadly, he never really recovered from the attack. At one point, his doctor, Allen Unger, left a message with my answering service to call him back. The service called me immediately at the *Dark Shadows* studio and I promptly returned the call. He said, "I'm so sorry about your car accident. How terrible that it happened at this time." I told him I had no idea what he was talking about, and he responded that my husband was very upset because he thought I had been hurt in an accident. Greg was apparently hallucinating and Dr. Unger said that I had to see Greg immediately to calm him down. So I got excused from the rehearsal, grabbed a cab and sped over to the hospital. I got there and he was thrilled to see me. He actually had to examine my face and hands however before he believed that I was okay—remember, he was a plastic surgeon. I then went back to the studio and taped the show. He was eventually transferred to a private room and stayed there through the rest of my time in *Shadows*.

One night when I walked over to Eleventh Avenue to hail a cab, I saw *DS* writer Gordon Russell waiting on the corner for a taxi. It was a tough time to get a cab, being rush hour, so we agreed to share the next one that came along. On the trip uptown, he complimented me on my interpretation of Megan, telling me how much he liked how I was developing the part. He also confided in me that when the role of Megan first came up, Dan Curtis had suggested getting me for the role. Gordon thought I was all wrong for the part; that I was much too dramatic for Megan, who he saw as the "girl next door," so he objected. Luckily for me, Dan had the final say and I did get the role. Gordon then said that he was glad I proved him wrong—that he was now very pleased that I was Megan. That meant a great deal to me because I respected his opinion and the compliment came unsolicited.

I truly enjoyed the character of Megan, my first straight role (ie: not a creature or a mad woman) on the show. Chris Bernau and I worked well together and he was fun to be with. We often ran into each other at our gym and had long conversations while we were going nowhere on our stationary bikes. But Megan didn't stay normal for too long. Barnabas got to me, bit me, and put me under his spell. In some scenes I had vampire fangs, and I would do anything Barnabas demanded of me. Toward the end, I even threw my husband off a cliff. I could be very nasty—or perhaps I should be more specific and say *Megan* could be. You can see that I ran the gamut on *Dark Shadows*—I started out as a monster created in a lab and ended up as a vampire. No other show could have given me that kind of experience.

All through the two years that I appeared on *DS,* I worked with the best actors in the business. Besides the ones I've already written about, I had the pleasure of acting with Joan Bennett, Kathryn Leigh Scott, Lara Parker, Nancy Barrett, Dennis Patrick, Louis Edmonds, David Henesy, Denise Nickerson, Diana Millay, Craig Slocum, Don Briscoe, and Michael Stroka. Since our storylines didn't coincide, I never worked on *DS* with Donna Wandrey, Jerry Lacy or Joel Crothers. (Jerry and I appeared in a Right Guard commercial during that time, and Joel and I were both on Episode 627 of *DS* but didn't have a scene together.) I hope I haven't left anyone out—everyone I worked with was fabulous.

It also was fun to receive a script and see who wrote it, since there were nine *DS* writers, the main ones being Sam Hall, Gordon Russell, Ron Sproat, and Art Wallace. Art had originally been commissioned by Dan Curtis to develop the story outline, and in addition wrote sixty-five episodes. But the beauty of *Dark Shadows* is that we have steadfast fans that have created a cult following, which helped to create a huge audience for the *DS* Festivals. These conventions are held every year, usually alternating between the coasts. They're wonderful for the actors in terms of being a reunion for all of us, and it's a great pleasure to see the old fans and meet the new ones.

Fans often ask me which of my *DS* characters was my favorite, and that's awfully hard to answer. I loved each character as I played her, and as is usual for me, I always think the part I'm playing at the moment is the best one ever. Eve's imperiousness, Jenny's vulnerability, Megan's adventurous nature, all were so different and extremely satisfying to work on. I'm pleased that I had the opportunity to play these diverse characters and to work with such a brilliant cast and crew. I could never have dreamed that more than thirty-five years later, *Dark Shadows* would be alive and well. Our characters live on, in the hearts of all our fans and at the Festivals. And the show lives on, on tape and DVD. *Dark Shadows* is recognized as one of the truly all-time great TV dramas.

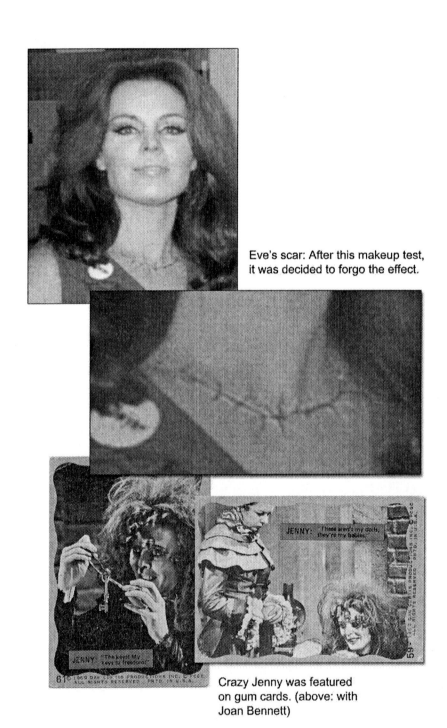

Eve's scar: After this makeup test,
it was decided to forgo the effect.

Crazy Jenny was featured
on gum cards. (above: with
Joan Bennett)

After Noon TV

September 50¢ Mac

"It's So Scary I Love It!"
DARK SHADOWS MAKES A MOVIE

THE OLD AND THE NEWER ED BAUER
Mart Hulswit of *The Guiding Light*
Bob Gentry of *A World Apart*

Are You The Most Interesting Viewer Of The Month?

SEE YOURSELF IN *AFTER NOON TV*

Marie Wallace and Nick Coster of *Another World-Somerset*

Somerset:
Vampire Lady Joins
Upper Middle Class

During my last day at the *Dark Shadows* studios, right after the run-through and before the dress rehearsal, I got a call from my agent, Jeff, about my next TV assignment. He asked if I'd like to audition for a new NBC daytime serial to be called *Somerset*. He added that the storylines might not be as exciting as *DS*, but that I would be creating a new character on a new show, which could be interesting. I jumped at the opportunity and responded, "Yes, I'd like to very much, 'cause they're putting a stake through my heart today!" I was playing Megan at that point and had become a vampire after Barnabas bit me. I was totally under his spell. I slept in a coffin, which was originally made for Nancy Barrett's character, and Nancy's just a little bit of a thing, so it wasn't very comfortable. In any event, Willie Loomis was going to end my misery that day, so it worked out very well. My agent's timing was impeccable.

The audition was the next day at the office of producer Lyle Hill. I was given the script when I arrived, and I read for him about twenty minutes later. Lyle asked me to keep the script, so I wasn't surprised when I got a call from my agent with a callback appointment on camera for the following day at an NBC studio. Greg was still recuperating in the hospital, and I was spending most of my free time with him. I didn't attempt to memorize the scene, because my mind was preoccupied with Greg and with doing everything possible to keep him comfortable. So, at the final audition, I was the only actress who held the script. I'm pretty adept at doing that so it looks very smooth and professional, but it was still apparent that I didn't know the lines. The next day, I was having a late lunch at Sardi's Restaurant with my friend Nancy Reardon when I got a call from my answering service. (It was one of the few restaurants in New York where they brought the phone to you at the table and I always got a kick out of that.) I had a message to call my agent, which I did immediately. He said that the producer really liked me above everyone else, but was afraid that I might have a problem with memorizing lines. Jeff assured him that I had a great memory, and I just hadn't concentrated on committing the script to memory because of my husband's condition. They were convinced and signed me up for the part of India Delaney.

Somerset was a spin-off from NBC's very popular soap *Another World.* It was the first daytime TV drama to produce a spin-off. They tried to keep us connected to *Another World,* even using the same theme music. The writers also worked the *Somerset* actors into a few scripts of *Another World,* to introduce us and get the audience interested in the new characters, and some characters would travel back and forth from Bay City to Somerset. They had two of the major characters from the original show move to the town of Somerset. They were Lahoma Vane Lucas (played by Ann Wedgeworth) and Sam Lucas (Jordan Charney). The initial stories revolved around all their new friendships. Henry Slesar, of *The Edge of Night,* was hired as the head writer, so it had a different tone than *Another World,* with more mystery, murder, and intrigue.

My first scene on *Another World* was in lawyer Sam's office. I was there to take care of some legal business, and the scene established me as a very rich, extremely powerful businesswoman. I had married into the powerful Delaney family, my husband being Robert Delaney (Nick Coster), son of Jasper Delaney, owner of Delaney Brands, the largest canning company in the Midwest. Jasper may have been the owner, but it was India who ruled the roost. In other words, I was the rich bitch, and in many ways, a direct descendant of *DS*'s Eve. India was a clever, crafty, shrewd woman who was determined to get everything she wanted. Poor Robert, her husband, didn't have a chance. She demeaned him whenever she had the chance, and even testified against him at his father's murder trial. Robert finally met and fell in love with a Riverboat Club singer, Jessica Buchanan (Wynne Miller) and decided to get a divorce. India always referred to Jessica sarcastically as "the little songbird" and was as mean to her as she was to anyone else. (What fun to play!) They were soon divorced and India then married Chuck Hillman (Ed Winters) who turned out to be worse than India.

We had marvelous actors in this soap, including Georgann Johnson, Paul Sparer, Gary Sandy, Ed Kemmer, Dorothy Stinnette, Alice Herson, Michael Lipton, Chris Pennock, and Joel Crothers. (*Dark Shadows* fans will remember Chris and Joel from their many roles on that show). Much of the rest of the cast was made up of Broadway stage actors. You don't see that as much today; many soap actors have no theatre experience at all.

Shortly after I signed the contracts for *Somerset,* I got a call from the *Dark Shadows* office offering me another part on the show. Naturally, I couldn't accept it, and I was perfectly comfortable with that, because *Somerset* was a long-term contract and my *DS* characters usually lasted for months and then got killed off. Henry Kaplan even called me and asked me to reconsider, but the dye had been cast. I was into the heart and mind of India. Then not long after that, Dan Curtis was producing the first movie based on *Dark Shadows,* and I was called about a part in the film. I gladly accepted, although they didn't have a shooting date for me. I was a little more than mad when I finally was called and the shoot dates coincided with my *Somerset* schedule. I tried to get Curtis to change my days, but there was no way that he could do that, and the producers of *Somerset* definitely weren't upsetting their schedule. It looked like *Dark Shadows* might now be out of my life, but of course, the *DS* Festivals changed all that (and they have become a very prominent part of nearly all the *DS* actors' lives).

Somerset was a complete change from *Dark Shadows.* In *DS,* actors were directed to be bigger than life. It was very much like being on the stage. *Somerset* was a more realistic show, and characters had to be played in a low-key manner. One of the great things about acting on television is that you can learn so much just by studying your own performances. In the first few weeks I watched, I wasn't pleased with what I saw and realized I had to tone my performances down. On most TV shows (except *DS*) movements, gestures, voice, and facial expressions have to be much smaller than they'd be on stage. The *Somerset* producer and directors were obviously satisfied because I didn't get any notes from them. Nonetheless, I knew that on television you have to be your own monitor, teacher, director, and critic (as my acting teacher, Wynn Handman, had taught all his students). TV directors have so many technical things to deal with, in a short period of time, that often they don't have time to work with the actors on the subtleties of acting.

Unlike *Shadows,* I started *Somerset* from the series' beginning, so I truly felt I was a part of a family. That really helped me too, because Greg came home from the hospital about a month after I started on the show, even though he wasn't fully recuperated. I felt that being in our home was so much better than staying in the hospital. He was more comfortable with that, too. There were times when I felt I should stay home with him but he encouraged me to keep working. And, in spite of how miserable he was, he enjoyed watching the show. He was always my biggest supporter, and even during his illness, he continued to give me emotional support. Of course, I arranged to have a private nurse with him whenever I was away from home and working at the studio.

During Greg's illness, he had always been optimistic, hopeful for a recovery, but one morning when I was leaving for City Island for a photo shoot for the cover of *Afternoon TV* magazine, Greg said, "I wish I could go with you." I felt encouraged for a moment and said, "So do I." But then he continued, "Yeah, I'd throw myself into the sea." For the first time, he wanted to give up. That tore me apart, and I hated to leave, but he insisted I go, so I kissed him and left.

When I returned home, I dismissed the nurse early, and just sat with Greg. He was sitting up in the bedroom in a big wingback chair, and all of a sudden he slumped over, and seemed to stop breathing. I kept shaking him and crying, "Greg, Greg, wake up." It was the first time since he was sick that I had cried in front of him. (I had always wanted to show my optimism and keep up his.) He suddenly looked up and said, "You're crying. Why are you crying?" And I said, "Because I feel so helpless. I don't know what to do for you." He answered, "Get me a shot of whiskey." He hardly ever drank hard liquor, but I suppose he thought it would stimulate him. I ran to the liquor cabinet, poured some in a glass, gave it to him, and he drank it down and seemed to feel better. We held each other and then he closed his eyes. He made a sound that I'd never heard before (later I realized it was the death rattle), and he was gone. As horrible as it was, I was grateful that we spent our last moments together in our own home. Luckily, most of my family members were in New York, and they were a great comfort to me.

I didn't want to do anything after that—not work, not play, anything. I took the first week off from work, and they rescheduled my shows. Once that week was over, I saw things more clearly, and I knew I would go back to the studio, to work, to life. Usually, the cast for the day gathered early in the morning in a coffee shop at West 72nd Street in Manhattan. A car service would pick us up there and drive us to the studio in Brooklyn (on 14th Street and Avenue M). But for my first morning back, the production office said they'd send the car to my home. What a surprise it was, when I went to the lobby and found Nick Coster (my husband on the show) waiting for me. The warm feeling of family was there, and I knew I was heading in the right direction.

I got back into the swing of things, and again was very comfortable at our studios in Brooklyn, although it was poles apart from our intimate *DS* studio. The *Shadows* studio in Manhattan was small, and ours was the only show that taped there, so we really took it over and made the place our own. The NBC studio was huge (it was originally a movie sound stage) and other shows were taped there at night. Also, during the day, *Another World* rehearsed and taped at one end of the building, while we were on the other end, and there was a great distance between us. When they taped at 2:45 p.m., however, we had to be very quiet on our side. Our taping followed immediately after theirs, but often we weren't even downstairs at that point. We would be in the makeup room, for last-minute touchups and for notes from the director. The two casts did mingle sometimes, most especially in the costume department and the makeup rooms, and it was fun to chat with old friends who

were on that show. My friend Connie Ford from *Nobody Loves an Albatross* is someone I'd see often, and that was always a delight. (She played Ada, the mother of
Another World's bad-girl character, Rachel.)

There was one day at the studio that I'll never forget, because I almost burned
the whole studio down! I was up on the fourth floor, lazing around on my LA-Z-
BOY recliner in my dressing room. I had lots of free time so I started a cup of tea
with an electric immerser that I put into a big plastic cup filled with water. The cup
was sitting on the carpeted floor because the cord wasn't long enough to reach up to
my dressing table, and I figured that it would just take a minute to heat up and then
I'd remove it from the floor. Then, over the sound system, I heard the floor manager
calling frantically, "Marie Wallace, where are you? Get down on the set immediately." So I flew down the stairs and realized that they had changed the blocking
schedule and were ready to block my entrance. We wasted no time and went right
into the scene, spending about twenty minutes on set, with my mind a million
miles away from my boiling cup of water. When we finished, I casually went back to
my dressing room. When I opened the door, there was black smoke everywhere,
and a small smoldering fire on the floor. I closed the door and ran to Nick Coster,
who saved the day by unplugging the cord, putting the fire out, opening the windows, and calming me down. The fire had contained itself within the cup, so the
carpet hadn't caught on fire, and after all the smoke left the room, you'd hardly have
known what happened, but it did take a few days for the smell to leave. I didn't do
any more "cooking" in my dressing room after that; I sent out for my teas instead!

I taped many, many *Somerset* episodes after that, with story lines constantly
changing, husbands changing (on the show, not in real life), and once more, a husband who was cheating on me and who tried to kill me. (That was Chuck, who hit
me over the head with a candlestick.) Just as when Eve was killed by Adam on *Dark
Shadows*, I lay around for a few days (that's in real time, since we taped it over several
days—in television time, it only took a short time for the ambulance to arrive). This
time, unlike my characters in *Dark Shadows*, India survived, but I decided to take a
long trip around the world. I told one of the characters as I was leaving that I'd send
a postcard saying, "Having a wonderful time. Glad you're not here." (Just for the
record, all those "I's" refer to India, not to Marie.) I taped my last show sometime in
1972 and decided it was a good chance for Marie (just like India) to go on a nice,
extended vacation, and then get back on the boards—the stage was calling.

The Women: Kim Hunter, Rhonda
Fleming, Alexis Smith, Dorothy
Loudon, and Marie Wallace
(with hairdresser Joe Tubens)

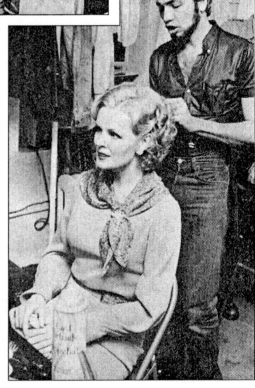

The Women:
How Catty Can You Get?

It was late morning on a Thursday in 1973, as I put the key into the door of my apartment, and I heard the phone ringing. I got the door opened, rushed to pick up the phone and it was Jeff Hunter, who had become my official agent when I signed the contract for *Somerset*. He was calling to say that he had arranged a last-minute audition for me for the first Broadway revival of Clare Boothe Luce's *The Women* (originally produced on Broadway in 1936), and it was for that day at 1 p.m.! I had just jogged home after a long workout at the health club, and certainly was in no shape for an audition. What's more, I always liked to take my time preparing, but instead, I became a bat out of hell. I hadn't read the play, but had seen the 1939 film and remembered the role of Crystal Allen—the femme fatale I was going in for—played by Joan Crawford, so I knew how I had to look for the audition. (The story revolves around the fact that glamorous Crystal breaks up the marriage of the wholesome leading character, Mary Haines.) I dressed and made up accordingly, and got myself to the rehearsal hall in record time. In fact, I was early, which is not surprising, actually, since that's part of my personality—I'm *always* on time, or early.

Now we're up to my entrance at the rehearsal hall. They were recasting the part of Crystal and the director, Morton DaCosta, had to do it *fast*. It was lunch break for the cast, but the director skipped lunch and used the time to audition a group of actresses. I had ten minutes to look over the script before I was called in, and the audition went very quickly. I couldn't tell how I'd done, but by the next morning, I got a call saying that DaCosta liked me very much and wanted me in the play. However, the producers, Jeremy Ritzer and Joel Key Rice, felt they needed another movie star for the part. They already had Alexis Smith—a Broadway star in *Follies* and other hits, and a Hollywood star as well; Rhonda Fleming and Myrna Loy, both movie stars making their Broadway debuts; Dorothy Loudon—the Broadway belter who went on to play Miss Hannigan in the original production of *Annie*; and Kim Hunter, the Oscar-winning actress who had become a Broadway star with her portrayal of Stella Kowalski in *A Streetcar Named Desire.*

The producers wanted to tout the production as having an "All-Star" cast. Crystal's actions are pivotal to the play and the director wanted me in the part, but if he couldn't have that, then at least he wanted me to be the standby for whatever star they would cast. Of course, *Dark Shadows* fans would have argued that I *was* a star, but these producers wanted another actress with an established Hollywood or Broadway name, and they seemed to have the final word. Almost! Lainie Kazan (known best as a singer at that time; she had replaced Barbara Streisand in *Funny Girl* on Broadway) was cast in the part, and as good a performer as she is, she was wrong for the part. One of the cast members was quoted saying about Kazan, in the *Daily News*, "Talented, sure, but dark, sultry, and buxom." In the film, Crawford played Crystal as a brunette, but Crystal was written as a sleek, blonde tigress, and so they tried to change Lainie by putting her in a blonde wig.

I didn't want to be a standby, but my agent was convinced that I would play the part eventually; in fact, he believed that by the time the show opened on Broadway, I'd be Crystal Allen. Since there weren't any other roles being offered to me at that point in time, and since it was such a delicious part, I accepted. Besides, I wanted to work with Morton DaCosta (known as *Tec* to most everyone), because I knew I could learn a great deal from him. He had directed a series of hits on Broadway including *Plain and Fancy, No Time for Sergeants, Auntie Mame, The Music Man, Saratoga,* and *The Wall.* He had also directed the film versions of *Auntie Mame* and *The Music Man,* and he had a reputation as one of the best directors in the country.

I soon heard the whole story about this production. The play had been fully cast, and rehearsals had begun earlier in the week, but one of the stars, Tammy Grimes, decided not to do the part of Crystal Allen. Actually, there had been a lot of drama that preceded these rehearsals. A year before, the producers had lined up Grimes, Alexis Smith, Myrna Loy, Julie Harris, and Maureen Stapleton for their production, with Ellis Rabb scheduled to direct. It took a long time for the producers to raise the capital for the show. There were three postponements of the opening, and they started losing their actors, who began taking other assignments. Then Rabb left to direct *A Streetcar Named Desire* at Lincoln Center. They then lost Julie Harris, which prompted Maureen Stapleton to quit, saying that if Julie wouldn't do it, she wouldn't either. Rosemary Harris and Eileen Heckart soon joined the cast, only to drop out because of the delays. When they were finally fully financed, Morton DaCosta was hired to direct.

I learned swiftly that as a standby, you don't get any rehearsal time until after the production has opened. During those first three-and-a-half weeks of rehearsals, you just watch, take notes, and learn the script. I'm a quick study, so I knew the part early on. Then, as luck would have it, Lainie got a bad cold and missed the last day of rehearsals before the out-of-town tryouts. A run-through was scheduled for the producers, and I jumped right in—without script in hand—and performed it. Aha! Now the producers knew what I could do.

Our tryouts were in Philadelphia at the Shubert Theatre and we opened to mixed reviews. When the play first appeared on Broadway in 1936, the critics panned it, but it went on to run for more than 600 performances, so no one seemed to be too upset about our reviews. Then, just three days before we were to go back to New York, Kazan was out of the picture. (The wrong casting seldom turns out favorably. Arthur Penn, the director I later worked with in *Sly Fox,* once said that eighty percent of his work was done if he cast the play correctly, but if an actor is wrong for the part, there's very little a director can do to change that.) The third producer, Lester Osterman, came in to Philly to see *The Women*, and he was convinced that I should have the part. The wardrobe mistress adjusted all of Lainie's costumes to fit me for my first night, and they started to make two new costumes to be ready for the opening in New York. So my agent's predictions came true; I was back on Broadway at the Forty-Sixth Street Theatre, opening on April 25, 1973.

The reviews in New York were again mixed, the main complaint being that the play was dated, although Edwin Wilson of the *Wall Street Journal* wrote, "It will probably please a great many theatergoers as it did in the past." There were many favorable comments for all the actresses, whether the critics liked the overall play or not:

"The play itself, in this era when the legend of Adam's rib has been displaced by the fervor of women's lib, is hopelessly out of date. Nevertheless, you should be entertained by Mrs. Luce's witty, venomous wisecracks, most of the acting, and the high Hollywood style in which the play has been directed and produced. The cast, under the capable direction of Morton DaCosta, is first-rate. Marie Wallace, playing the seductive and predatory Crystal, makes it altogether clear why men leave wives at sight of her."—George Oppenheimer, *Newsday.*

"It is the dated quality, however, that somehow gives *The Women* its charm. As for the stars, they will evoke memories, and each member of the audience will have its favorite. I was delighted with Marie Wallace's almost Jean Harlow performance as climbing and gold-digging Crystal. She only stepped into the role very recently and gives so much to the evening."—William A. Raidy, *Newhouse Newspapers.*

Other critics praised it without reservations:

"I loved every tinsel moment of it. The all-star cast of women is sheer delight…. Marie Wallace is a delightful surprise as a vicious salesgirl."—Emory Lewis, *The Record.*

"It is Bravo and Bouquets to the women of Clare Boothe Luce's vintage classic. The wit, sparkle and bulls-eye characterizations are as intact today as freshly opened champagne…and Marie Wallace, the understudy who last night became a star, is excellent as the husband-stealing siren."—Virginia Woodruff, *WMCA Radio.*

"So marvelously bitchy from beginning to end that it's thoroughly enjoyable and continually funny. *The Women* is like watching hungry cats prowling around each other's territory, arching their backs, always ready to spring. Marie Wallace, in her first starring role, is absolutely superb as the hard-as-diamonds tramp who wins her victories in the hay."—Leonard Probst, *NBC Radio.*

I'm certain that it would have been a great deal more satisfying if I had been in the play from the beginning, rehearsing every day, working with all the actors during that discovery phase. In many ways, those are the best times of all; experimenting, trying new approaches, and taking chances on the interpretation. But when an actor goes into a play just before the opening, she has to conform to so much that was decided beforehand, and the rapport that is built up between actors during those three or four weeks of rehearsal just isn't there. It's unquestionably less fun, but I was still very pleased to be playing the part. And it was truly a brilliant production. It had the proportions of a musical, with scenic designs by Oliver Smith, fabulous costumes by Ann Roth and Ray Diffen, and was, in all probability, the last straight (non-musical) show with such a huge cast: twenty-four.

Today, a writer has to limit his cast to five or six, with one set, or he doesn't get produced—it's prohibitively expensive otherwise. Our production cost $350,000 to mount, and another $50,000 was raised to keep it running. That meant it was the most expensive non-musical ever delivered to Broadway at that time, but these days, that's chicken feed. Now a simple Off-Broadway show can cost three times that amount. Still, Crystal *was* a delectable role, and I even got a chance to take a bubble bath on stage. It was all just an illusion—no water or even soap bubbles, just bubble *wrap* that was tucked into my Merry Widow (a strapless brasselette), and after a few weeks of the same wrap, I think I came out of my *bath* dirtier than when I went in. Another Broadway revival of the play was done in 2001, and they used a real bathtub and water, but we weren't about to get that realistic in 1973.

For some reason, the show didn't quite make it. Our audiences loved it, but not enough of them came. The producers didn't think we could get through the summer, since Broadway didn't yet have that wonderful organization called TKTS (ticket booths where Broadway and Off-Broadway tickets are sold at half price). That would have helped us tremendously, since the word-of-mouth was good, and if enough people saw it and spoke about it, we might have had full houses at full price by September. But that's all speculation, and the reality is that we ran for a mere few months and closed on June 17. Our last performance was a Sunday matinee, and I wanted desperately to be somewhere else, but I couldn't miss our final show. My thoughts were over on the East Side in a hotel where my best girlfriend, Nancy Reardon, was getting married to Tom Flynn. I had to miss the ceremony and most of the party. I ran out of that theatre without even saying my final goodbyes to the cast (again the proverbial bat out of hell), because I wanted to see the bride and groom before they left the party, and I wanted to be part of the party, too. And I did and I was, so it all ended on a happy note. I'm just a party girl at heart.

I was a *Jean Harlow blonde* during the run and for a while after. Did I have more fun? I'm not sure about that, but the look was striking, and sometimes, as I walked down the street, friends would pass me right by, not recognizing me. That's how much it changed my look. I love changes, so that was great, and I might have kept that color much longer, but two things convinced me otherwise. When I got up in the morning and looked in the mirror, I didn't look like me—I felt I looked dull, that I really needed makeup to look good. But as a redhead without makeup, I had all the color I wanted, and was always pleased with my reflection. And more important, keeping the lighter color was extremely harsh on my hair. I couldn't bear to see dark roots, so I kept going back to the beauty shop to have them bleached, and I did it once too often. One morning, I found clumps of blonde hair on my pillow and I said, "Enough!" I went back to my red hair, and once more felt like Marie. Redheaded Marie, just recently the toast of Broadway and an overnight "star," once more back at the starting square in the theatre game of Life.

Co-stars (from top):
Betsy von Furstenberg,
Estelle Parsons, Bert Lahr,
and Ron August

Mert & Phil

After I left *Somerset*, commercial auditions and bookings took up some of my time, along with theatre auditions. One of the auditions turned out to be for *Mert & Phil*, a new drama by Anne Burr. It was to be the opening play of the 1974-75 New York Shakespeare Festival's second season at Lincoln Center, with Joseph Papp as the director and executive producer, and Bernard Gersten as the associate producer. The scenic design would be by Santo Loquasto with costumes by Theoni Aldredge—a very impressive group.

Auditioning for *Mert & Phil* was quite an interesting experience. I picked up my character's scene and studied it for a few days. My appointment with Joe Papp was at the Public Theatre on Lafayette Street in Greenwich Village. I did the scene for him with another actress, and when I finished, he said that he liked my reading but it was precisely what he'd expect the character to do. He wanted her to be different. Papp always went for different, offbeat, opposite-to-the-character interpretations. He often thought *different* was *better*, but, in my opinion, that wasn't always true. He wanted me to take a completely different approach, one he had thought up for the part, and he asked me to return the next day and read it with that in mind. I felt that what he asked me to do was very wrong for the character, but I said, "Why not? I can try it." And that's exactly what I did at the next audition. And lo and behold, when it was over, he said, "You were right the first time. Forget what I said." I then read a little more with my original ideas, and left the theatre. This time, I was confident in my audition and as I expected, his office called my agent offering me the part, which I was very happy to accept.

We rehearsed at the Public Theatre, and on the first day, I met Anne Burr and all the actors. I was delighted to see Estelle Parsons (I knew her from the gym at the 92nd Street Y), Beverlee McKinsey (*Another World*'s villainess Iris Carrington), and Michael Lombard (I always saw him running around the Central Park reservoir when I was out for a run, but we had never worked together). The cast was rounded out with Rhoda Gemignani, Norman Ornellas, and Marilyn Roberts, with George Dzundza as Michael's standby. (George went on to a great TV and movie career, which is still going strong).

The three weeks of rehearsals breezed by, and next thing I knew it was September 26, and we were on our way to Pennsylvania. We unpacked and settled into our hotel rooms, and then Estelle and I looked for the local Y and made arrangements to use the pool and gym. We also bought flowers and vases for our room, because the hotel accommodations were pretty drab. Our out-of-town try-outs were at the Annenberg Center for Communication Arts and Sciences' Zellerbach Theatre, at the University of Pennsylvania. It was almost identical to the Lincoln Center stage where we were scheduled to open in New York, so it was a good stage for us to work on. Because it was a university theatre, there were Q&As many nights with Joe Papp and the audience. Most of us didn't want to go out on stage for the sessions but we had no choice. We were uncomfortable as we could sense that much of the audience didn't like the play—the hisses and boos helped us figure that out! One night someone in the audience said, "Why don't you produce plays like the ones Eugene O'Neill and Tennessee Williams wrote?" And Papp answered, "I'd produce them, if they were being written today, but unfortunately, they're not. I produce the most contemporary plays. If you can send any to me, I'd be happy to read them."

In fairness to the play, there were many in the audience who loved it and felt it was a very important piece of work. Marilyn Stasio, drama critic for *Cue* magazine, wrote (after the New York reviews), "Burr was violently denounced by critics who still cherish the very values she is questioning. Neither evil nor vindictive men, the critics illustrated an imbalanced and limited perception. They were caught off-guard by an attack on values they hold dear and are afraid or unwilling to question themselves. And the playwright, whatever the artistic flaws of this play, was denied the encouragement, respect, and admiration she has at the very least deserved."

It was the subject matter that was hard to take. It's a play about physical disintegration, starting with Mert, a working-class woman, who is recovering from a mastectomy. It was very timely since Happy Rockefeller and Betty Ford had recently gone public about their battles with breast cancer and the disease was very much in the news, although Anne had written it two years before our knowledge of their illnesses. Mert is anguished by what society has led her to perceive as the loss of her identity, and she explodes in anger. As the writer said in an interview with Tom Topor of the *New York Post*, "The play is about loss, decline, and decay—Phil's as well as Mert's. Everybody's."

We did our two weeks of tryouts in Philadelphia and then headed back to New York and moved into the Vivian Beaumont theatre. It was much newer than most theatres, so the dressing rooms were really great. Many theatre owners, even when they refurbish the entire front of the house and audience area, never touch the dressing rooms, and they're as dreary as can be. So it was a pleasure for each of us to have our own large, clean, pretty room, complete with bathroom and shower. Working in live theatre, you learn to be grateful for small things. We did fourteen previews starting on October 14, and then opened for the critics on October 30.

My role was the Beauty Lady, and was a fun role in the midst of a very black comedy. Picture this: The play opens in a hospital room with Mert (Estelle) in the bed. She is recovering from a mastectomy, her twenty-year marriage is on the rocks, she is very depressed, and is an alcoholic on top of that. The next scene is at home, and we discover that her mother-in-law, played by Marilyn Roberts, lives with them. Mert's husband Phil (Lombard) is still on the scene. Mom is pretty old, and she's incontinent. But that's okay; Mert has figured a way to get her to the bathroom in a New York minute. The old gal wears roller skates all the time so that when nature calls, Mert just rolls her to the bathroom.

The apartment is pretty messy to begin with, and Mert gets more and more slovenly as time goes by. She drinks a lot of beer, and when she finishes with the cans, she simply throws them on the floor. When the story is in full-bloom rage, the doorbell rings. Mert, dressed in a ratty old housecoat and slip, reluctantly answers it, and she finds the Beauty Lady—that's me. I look like a perfect Avon Lady: hair simply and beautifully coifed, with not a strand out of place, flawless makeup, and wearing a lovely, crisp, aqua dress—the appearance of perfection itself. In my polite way, I force myself through the door and go straight to the center of the sofa and take my seat. I end up between roller-skated Mama on my right, and, on my left, drunken and disheveled Mert. (Throughout the scene, blissfully ignored by the Beauty Lady, Mama coughs, spits on the floor, wipes it with the toe of her skate, and takes hits off her bottle of bourbon.) Oblivious to the squalor and incongruity of the situation, I go right into my sales pitch, never seeming to take a breath or a pause. "And here's our brand new line of Kissy Kolors, moisturizer-and-lip-bloom-in-one-with-a-Sateen-Sheen, I'm wearing it myself this is Yes-Yes-Me (sticking my lips out prettily), of course these, as all our products are totally non-hypo-allergenic-free now I did have all these in sample size but they go so *fast* do you prefer the Hot Hot Red or the Pithy Pink?" I even try to sell to the old lady, giving her a tiny plastic tube of the Pithy Pink lipstick.

At one point, old Mama starts interrupting and talking dirty, and Mert gets up, grabs a huge hollow plastic mallet, and boinks the old one's head. Mom knows what's coming, grabs her crash helmet from under the sofa and throws it on her head. My character is still unaware of the surroundings, fully focused on her products, and goes rattling on. It's actually one of the funniest scenes in the play, and a relief from all the madness, as some of the critics pointed out:

"The play picks up when Mert is visited by an Avon lady, who blithely recites her fancy monologue, (with its prize word, 'non-hypo-allergenic free' and its refrain 'I use it myself') to a bemused Mert and her raucous mother-in-law."—Henry Popkin, *Herald Statesman*, Yonkers.

"Marie Wallace appears for a scene as a seller of beauty preparations who wisely flees from the mad family, and she supplies one of the few attractive interludes."—Richard Watts.

"The Beauty Lady is played by the fetching and statuesque Marie Wallace [and] she is nice to have around."—Douglas Watt, *Daily News*

It was a pleasure to work with Estelle Parsons and Michael Lombard; they're real pros. And I would love to have seen George Dzundza play the part of Phil once or twice since he's such a good actor, but Michael never missed a performance, so that didn't happen. Papp was nice, but he wasn't much of a director. His fame came as a producer, and he was truly great at that. I think it was a good play that was presented in the wrong theatre. I'm sure that the New York Shakespeare Festival at Lincoln Center lost half of their subscribers because of the production, since the subscribers at that theatre, being of a certain age, preferred the more traditional plays. Many of the critics shared that half of the audience's sentiments, including *WNEW-TV*'s Stewart Klein who expressed his "sympathy for any theatergoer who might be tempted to burn down the theatre, and producer-director Papp along with it."

At the same time we were playing, Papp and Gersten presented *Richard III*, starring Michael Moriarty, at the Mitzi E. Newhouse Theatre, part of the Lincoln Center complex. That should have been in the Beaumont, and our play at the Newhouse. In the smaller Newhouse, audiences might have accepted our play as an *experimental* piece. In any event, our play was set to run for a limited period and we got through it, closing on December 8, after forty-one performances. Perhaps it was way before its time, and if someone produced it today, it might be a smash hit. As for me, it was a lovely experience, and another *beauty part*.

Meadow Brook Theatre

Early one morning, in the spring of '76, just as I was leaving for a jog in Central Park, my agent called asking if I'd like to audition for *Born Yesterday*, a revival being done at the Meadow Brook Theatre. I figured he meant Meadow Brook, Long Island, but he said, "No, Meadow Brook, Rochester." "Ah," I said, "Rochester, N.Y.," whereupon he said, "No, Rochester, Michigan." I'd never heard of that Rochester, but the thought of working on the character of Billie Dawn intrigued me and I answered in the affirmative. I went out to Central Park and jogged right to the Drama Book Shop where I bought a copy of the play and proceeded to work on it. I usually read a play through three or four times, and then I start from the beginning and circle all my speeches with a black marker. I continue to read from beginning to end slowly, absorbing everything, jotting down any ideas that pop into my head. Without consciously trying to memorize, I eventually become immersed in the part and know most of the script.

The audition, run by Terence Kilburn, was a few days later at the Actors' Equity rehearsal hall. Terry began his career as a child actor in Hollywood, appearing in over fifty films, including *Goodbye Mr. Chips, A Christmas Carol, Lolita,* and *National Velvet.* In 1970 he became Artistic Director of the Meadow Brook, and he ran it very successfully until 1994, when he retired. He conducted the audition, although the play was to be directed by Anthony Mockus.

I had a callback within a few days, and nine days later, I had the part and was on a plane to Detroit. I was met on arrival by the stage manager and driven to Oakland University (the six-hundred-seat theatre is part of the drama department of the university, and is Michigan's largest professional theatre). I was taken to my living quarters, which turned out to be a trailer, and a very nice one, indeed. There were about twelve of these trailers, and they housed all of the actors. Each trailer had two bedrooms, a living room, and a kitchen. Some of the actors shared a trailer, and it was certainly set up to be comfortable that way, but my agent arranged for me to have the entire trailer to myself. I like to be alone when I'm working on a part, especially one that size. (After the first three minutes, Billie is on stage for the remainder of the play.)

I met many of the actors that day in the trailer court, and we began rehearsals bright and early the next morning. The play, written by Garson Kanin, is about junk tycoon Harry Brock, who arrives in Washington with his naïve mistress, ex-chorus girl Billie Dawn. He tries to use her as a tool in his corrupt deals, but Billie's uneducated manners are an embarrassment even to the crude Brock, so he hires a reporter, Paul Verrall, to tutor her. The complications begin when Billie blooms under Paul's attention and turns out to be a lot smarter than her sugar daddy. Of course, Paul falls in love with her. It's a marvelous Pygmalion story, filled with laughs; and with the very talented group of actors they had assembled, I knew we'd have a good show. Guy Stockwell, who worked continuously in films and TV from the forties through the nineties, and ran a theatre company in L.A., played Brock. Peter Brandon, who was a very experienced stage actor, played the reporter. The rest of the cast included Cheryl Giannini, Fred Thompson, Dan C. Bar, Edgar Meyer, James D. O'Reilly, and Marianne Muellerleile. Timing is everything in comedy, and I saw immediately that these actors had it, so I relaxed and knew it was going to be an enjoyable seven weeks.

From the day I arrived, we had the most turbulent Michigan weather, with tornadoes, crippling ice storms, and bizarre snowstorms with green lightning. It didn't matter; I could weather every storm because working in regional theatre is so stimulating and challenging. You're given a full three-and-a-half weeks of rehearsals, and then you have the same amount of time to perform. I love being away from the everyday concerns at home; appointments, auditions, subways and buses, traffic, and phone calls (except the ones from a boyfriend; they're always welcomed). You can throw yourself into the work, the place, and the socializing with the cast, and it's extremely gratifying. Trailer living was fine, except every once in a while it didn't work quite as well as staying in a hotel room. On one of my days off, I decided to give my hair and scalp an oil treatment. I applied all the oils, waited the required twenty-five minutes, stepped into the tub, and turned on the shower. The water was coming out nice and hot, I lathered up, and in a very short time, the water turned ice cold. I hadn't thought of the limited supply of hot water in a trailer. I jumped out of that tub, started heating water, and I spent the rest of the day trying to get rid of the oil. Some day off! After that, I found a little beauty shop on the campus, and went there for my hair treatments.

The winter wonderland ice storm that season was a little scary. Once it started, I thought that I'd better get some food supplies, so I took a trip to the market with the trailer manager. I had a driver's license but almost never got behind the wheel so he was driving. The road was a sheet of ice, which I hadn't expected, but the store wasn't too far away, so I thought we could manage it. When we got to the parking lot, he kept circling around, and passing open parking spots. I finally asked why he didn't take one of those. He then said, "I have no peripheral vision, so I can only park where I can drive straight in and out." Oh, boy, was I in trouble! Luckily, we got back safe and sound, but snowdrifts were quickly accumulating. A beautiful huge tree that I loved, outside my window, with branches that spread over my roof, was now filling with foot-long ice cycles, and it looked like it just might collapse over my tiny abode. We then experienced power failure in the trailers, and a few minutes later, there was a knock on the door, and we were being evacuated. It turned into an interesting adventure because they brought us to Meadow Brook Hall, the original one-hundred-room Tudor mansion of Oakland University's benefactors, Mr. And Mrs. Alfred G. Wilson, and we spent the night there. We relished every moment of it, enjoying the fine furnishings and art objects, which were a far cry from our humble trailers.

A few days after the storm subsided, when I was back in my trailer, I was listening to the radio and suddenly there was an interruption in the music with an announcement that a tornado was heading our way. The announcer insisted that we should open all our windows to let the wind blow through the house, and he advised us to go to the basement. There was only one problem: I didn't have a basement! We were lucky. The tornado skipped our area, but it devastated the next town. We happened to take a ride there the next day, only to find roofs torn off buildings and many trees destroyed. I began to feel fortunate that my permanent home was in the Northeast where we have mild winters in comparison to the Midwest.

The weather calmed down by the time we opened, and I enjoyed my days off and the performances at night. The audiences there were enthusiastic and supportive, and we had a brilliant, sold-out-every-night run. This engagement didn't end after the usual seven weeks. We did a tour, which was sponsored by the Michigan Council of the Arts. We finished playing on a Sunday afternoon and the tour was to begin on Wednesday. I thought that was a great opportunity to run into New York to see my then-boyfriend, so I flew out on Sunday night, with plans to return early Wednesday morning. What a mistake! Wednesday at 6 a.m., on my way to the airport, I couldn't see my hand in front of me because the fog was so thick. We got to LaGuardia Airport easily (those New York cab drivers can drive through anything), but my 7 a.m. flight was postponed for an hour. Then it was delayed yet another hour, and another. I kept calling the theatre with updates, and I was getting more and more nervous by the minute. I was due at the theatre for a run-through at 1 p.m., after which we were to leave by two vans for our first performance. (We were scheduled to play a different Michigan city each of the next eight nights: Brighton, Owosso, Grand Haven, Coldwater, Roscommon, Cheboygan, Calumet, and Escanaba.) The fog finally lifted, and I boarded the plane and flew to Detroit, where a theatre crewmember was waiting for me with his car engine running. We flew (this time in his car) to the campus, and went directly backstage. I heard my first cue a second later; timing is everything. The (male!) stage manager was in the wings, script in hand, ready to go on for me, and I just stepped in front of him and made my entrance, without losing a beat. Believe me, from that day forward, I always arranged to arrive at my destination one full day earlier than I was expected on stage.

I had a ball at Meadow Brook playing Billie Dawn, so when I saw the announcement that the second play of the following season was to be Tennessee Williams' *The Night of the Iguana*, I knew I wanted to play Maxine. I had played the part years before at the Hampton Playhouse (in New Hampshire) when I was much too young for the role, and I felt that I was really ready for her now. I called Terry Kilburn and told him that I wanted to audition for it. He responded that I didn't have to audition for them any more; they knew my work and liked it. But the director, Charles Nolte, didn't know me, and Maxine was so completely different than Billie, I was afraid they'd think I couldn't play such an earthy character. I wanted to guarantee that I'd get the part and I also wanted the new director to choose me, not inherit me.

When they came to New York to audition, I was called and a time was set up. Two days before my appointment, I was hit with the worst cold; it was bad enough to send me to bed. By Thursday, I wasn't coughing, but my voice was affected and was down in the gutter. I was ready in every other way. I had put together a great outfit for the audition—basically the same as I had fashioned for my first Maxine. It was simple; just jeans and a top worn open to the waist, exactly what Maxine would wear. I dragged myself to the studio, sipping hot tea with lemon and honey. The adrenaline kicked in and I did a good reading. In fact, the low gravelly voice worked to my advantage, helping my characterization of this down-to-earth character. The whole package worked, and I got cast in the part and took off for Rochester once again.

Charles Nolte turned out to be as good and as sensitive a director as he is an actor. He had starred on Broadway in four plays; was very well known for his portrayal of the title role in *Billy Budd,* and he won the 1950 Theatre World Award for his part in *Design for a Stained Glass Window.* I also learned that Charles (Chuck) had adapted and staged the original Meadow Brook production of Charles Dickens' *A Christmas Carol* years before, and as recently as 2004, it was still being presented there. (In the 1938 Hollywood movie, Terry played

Tiny Tim.) Chuck also cast *Iguana* very well. A teacher from the university played Hannah, and it was hard to believe that she wasn't pursuing an acting career—she was so good. They also brought popular TV actor David Canary in from New York. He's had a great career since *Iguana,* winning five Emmy Awards for playing Adam Chandler on *All My Children* over the years. It was fun to renew my acquaintance with David. We had done the same play together at the Hampton Playhouse, but I just had one scene with him then, as he played Hank, the bus driver. Now he had the lead role of Shannon, the defrocked clergyman on the verge of a breakdown. Almost all of his scenes were with Hannah, a middle-aged spinster, and me (Maxine, the gutsy owner of the Costa Verde Hotel where Shannon finds refuge). David was a delight to work with, bringing so many nuances to the role. It was a talented group of actors, and we became a great ensemble.

During the run, one of the actresses came to me with a book she had been reading to show me that the author had referred to me several times. Actors get used to seeing their names in press releases, reviews, and magazine articles, but this was a novel, so we were all surprised. The book was *Praise the Human Season* by Don Robertson, and it's a really lovely story. It was a pleasure to read and especially to find the main characters, the Ambersons, talking about me:

> "The Ambersons watched a great deal of television. They were especially fond of daytime serials, and Amberson's favorite was one called *Somerset....* He became interested in the female villain, whose character name was India Delaney. She had high cheekbones and she was, in Amberson's opinion, a beautiful woman—and forget her character deficiencies."

A few pages later it continues:

> "Her name" said Anne Amberson, "is Marie Wallace."

They continue talking about me, and then Mr. Amberson says,

> "Somehow I don't see her as a Marie. She is too imperious for such a name."
> "You see her as a Regina," said Anne.
> "All right. Perhaps I do. But what I mean to say is the name 'Marie' calls to mind dime-store clerks."
> "I'm sure Marie Antoinette would be delighted to hear that."

They then get into other subjects and their story continues, but I must say I got a real kick out of reading it.

The November weather cooperated with us, and this time the only lightning flashes that we saw were on stage, when Tennessee Williams' vivid characters came to life. It was a truly exciting, passionate, and poetic production. When I arrived back in New York, *Iguana* was playing at the Circle in the Square's 681-seat house. I went to see it and I didn't think it came near to the production values we had in Michigan. The Broadway theatre was only slightly larger than the Meadow Brook, but they spent many times more money to mount it than we did. I wished that New York audiences could have been transported to Nolte's Michigan production. I believe anyone who saw both would agree that ours was better.

Regional theatre experience is a must for all actors, and I would especially encourage young actors to seek out work in the best of these theatres around the country. The actor gets to play really good roles in important plays and gets support and encouragement from the audience and the production staff. He or she is then ready, once again, to go back to New York and knock the audiences' socks off.

Sly Fox: Marie with two "great ones" — Jackie Gleason and Cleavon Little

Sly Fox:
How Sweet It Was!

Sly Fox, based on Ben Jonson's comic classic, *Volpone,* and written by Larry Gelbart (*M*A*S*H*), had a successful run on Broadway that started in December 1976, with George C. Scott. Gretchen Wyler played the part of Miss Fancy beautifully and I remember thinking that it would be a good part for me. Before the show closed in February 1978, the Shubert Organization had already decided to produce it again, as a major road show starring Jackie Gleason. The plan was to stop touring once we hit Ft. Lauderdale, Florida, open the theatre season there and stay for a few weeks, and then move to Broadway. It was a big deal, with financing that topped the original Broadway production, and they treated it just that way, with a four-week rehearsal period in Florida and a week of previews in San Diego before the official opening date of March 9, 1978.

But let's start at the beginning, which, as always, was the audition process. Guess what? Shades of *Dark Shadows,* this casting director, Shirley Rich, didn't think I was right for the part for which my agent submitted me ("too elegant," she said). Casting directors have a way of pigeonholing an actor into certain types of roles, especially if they've seen the actor in a part that he portrayed very well. (I'm sure she saw me in many plays, but the part of Mrs. Garland, a most elegant lady, in *The Right Honourable Gentleman* was the one she remembered the best.) Ms. Rich also told my agent she was extremely busy with other auditions, and didn't have any time slots left. But my agent was still the persistent Jeff Hunter, and he managed to squeeze in an interview/audition for me, at the beginning of Ms. Rich's lunch break.

The character was the one I liked when I originally saw the play, Miss Fancy, an earthy, flamboyant madam. (My favorite line came in a courtroom scene when Miss Fancy answers the question about the kind of work she does with, "I think of myself as a pleasure engineer.") I met the casting director and read, and she told me that she thought I was too upscale for the part. However, she liked my reading and set up an audition with the director in spite of her misgivings as to my type. The audition was on stage at a Broadway theatre (often they're in a rehearsal studio or an office). I always preferred to audition on stage, so I was comfortable going into the audition. I dressed for the part (sexy), and was prepared to audition with another actor, but our casting director was there and I had to read with her—which is not as easy as working with an actor. It was especially difficult in the scene I had to read, because it was Miss Fancy's seduction of old man Crouch, a miserly millionaire, and Ms. Rich didn't exactly fit that part. To her credit, she made it as comfortable for me as was possible under the circumstances—she set up the scene with two chairs, with her back to the audience and my chair facing straight out. The director, Arthur Penn, was in the middle of the auditorium, and about three quarters of the way through the reading, he started talking (I wasn't sure to whom), and walking toward the stage. I finally heard him say, "It's okay, Marie, you don't have to read anymore, you're terrific! Can you come back in an hour to read with the actors I'm considering for another role?" That's usually a very good sign. It means the director likes the actress reading and wants to pair her up with the right actor. While it wasn't a sure bet that I would win the part, I knew I had a good chance and was delighted to return.

The stage manager gave me the full script, and I went over to Actors' Equity lounge, found a nice quiet corner, and sat there for the next forty-five minutes, concentrating on my scenes and staying focused. I was raring to go when I got back to the theatre. I read with three other actors; Mr. Penn thanked me, and I left. Within a day, Jeff received an offer on my behalf for the part, and after a little negotiating, we accepted.

I'm always happy to sign a contract for a show but when I heard this cast list, I got truly excited. I already knew that TV legend Jackie Gleason was set to play the lead role, but I hadn't known that Cleavon Little (already famous for his role as Bart, the sheriff in 1974's *Blazing Saddles)* was going to play Simon Able, Gleason's sidekick and accomplice. I got keyed up about going to Florida to start our rehearsals and started packing for the long tour. The cast and I left soon after that for Ft. Lauderdale. Instead of the usual New York rehearsal, the rehearsal location was arranged for Gleason's convenience, near his home. These rehearsals were different than any I'd done before. Jackie didn't have an understudy (if he was sick, the show just wouldn't go on), but he did have a sort-of stand-in (more like the movies). Since Gleason loved to play golf more than anything, after about an hour or two of rehearsals, on any given day, he would walk to the door (already dressed in his golf outfit), turn around and say, "So long, pals," and leave. Then the stand-in would take his place and the rehearsals would continue. The first time he did it, I thought it was a joke, but he meant business. He knew his lines from day one, and he had figured out what stage business he'd do, so I guess he felt that there was no need for him to be there until the director blocked a new scene. This was not exactly the way stage actors usually work, but it was quite acceptable to management for such a megastar. (He had a long, impressive career, but he's probably best remembered today for his leading role as the grouchy New York City bus driver Ralph Kramden in the 1950s TV classic *The Honeymooners*.) When he worked on television, he knew exactly what he wanted to do, and he did it. He liked to surprise his fellow actors because he thought that created spontaneity, but stage actors have a slightly different take on that. Still, he was the boss, referred to in the industry as The Great One, so he was never questioned. He was a great comic; it's just that he had work habits very different from a typical stage actor.

We all had one, two, or three scenes with Jackie, but Cleavon and Gleason were on stage together throughout the play. However, until we got to San Diego (our first stop on the tour), Jackie spent very little time rehearsing with Cleavon. Because of this, Cleavon was ready to quit the show completely, and I don't know how our director made sure he stayed, but I'm so glad he did, because he was spectacular in his role, and extraordinary as a person. In San Diego, Gleason finally got down to business and the play started to pull together. We did previews there, with the full cast finally in place, and it worked! I guess Jackie knew what he was doing all along.

While we were in San Diego, I learned that when the producers were originally planning the first Broadway production, they sent the script to Gleason before any other actor, and that he turned it down because he had decided never to do another Broadway show. In fact, he sent it back without even reading it, because years before he had a terrible experience with producer David Merrick. (That had all happened during the 1959 Broadway production of *Take Me Along*, for which Jackie won a Tony Award. Merrick and Gleason had big differences of opinion about everything and had public verbal fights that were written up in the daily papers—each of them topping the insults of the other.) The Shuberts took another chance and sent the script to him again, and this time he said yes. I once asked why he did it this time and he said, "I made the mistake of opening the envelope and reading the play, and then I couldn't turn it down." I was glad he accepted because we had a wonderful, first-class tour set up. After San Diego, we went to San Francisco and played there for eight weeks.

In a major road show, there are a number of openings and consequently, there are lots of reviews. And most of the critics loved the play, the cast, and The Great One:

"[*Sly Fox*] abounds with funny lines, expertly delivered by an uncommonly talented cast....Gleason is an almost matchless comic actor....Cleavon Little nearly equals Gleason as an actor....Marie Wallace is a very alluring and seductive Miss Fancy...a saucy Miss Fancy, who refers to herself as a *pleasure engineer* and would stop at nothing—and doesn't—to get Fox's name on a marriage contract."—Bill Hagen, *Evening Tribune*

"Every player, from bit to big, is right on the mark and director Arthur Penn has staged it with cunning hilarity."—Glenna Syse, *Chicago Sun-Times*

"In supporting roles, the play is rich with well-played and very amusing characterization. Marie Wallace as Miss Fancy, a well-to-do hooker who wants to marry Foxwell Sly is perfectly wonderful as a part Mae West and part Delilah. Not only is Miss Wallace lovely to look at, her talent is obviously apparent. She is sort of a bawdy Eve Arden."—*San Francisco's Gay Weekly*

'The rest of the cast is excellent without exception. Irwin Corey shuffles along perfectly as Crouch. His scene with Miss Fancy, in which she buries his hand in her ample bosom and he gets so excited he dodders off to sleep, is one of the show's great moments."—William C. Glackin, *The Sacramento Bee*

Lots of opening nights meant lots of opening-night parties. At one of the festivities in San Francisco, Jackie called me over to his table to introduce me to his friend, sports legend Joe DiMaggio. It was kind of fun, especially when he said to DiMaggio, "Joe, this is a great dame. You ought'a marry her. She is to the Theatre, what you used to be to Baseball." That was a fabulous compliment and I relished it. However, I had a boyfriend in New York so I wasn't interested. (At that point, it was eight years since my husband had died, and as difficult as it was, I had started dating again a few years before the tour.) Joe DiMaggio may not have been interested either, but it was an entertaining thought.

It was on this tour that I started taking pictures on a regular basis. My camera wasn't anything special—just a simple point-and-shoot that I had bought for myself as a birthday present. I had lots of opportunities to take interesting candid photos and group shots in the dressing rooms, especially on opening nights, and then later at the first-night parties. However, it started to get embarrassing, because the camera often seemed to jam or malfunction just as I'd get Jackie and a group of his friends to pose. His guests were always big stars. Jack Haley (The Tin Man in *The Wizard of Oz*) was there one night when I screwed up. When it was the flash that wouldn't fire, it was very noticeable to the group, so I'd apologize and say I'd be back. I used to have phone conversations with my boyfriend, Bob, every night, and I'd go through the camera problems I'd had that day. He had worked his way through school as a photographer and was quite an expert, but he couldn't help too much because the problem was mostly due to the sub-par equipment. Happily, when we were playing in Chicago, I had another birthday, and he came out to visit me with a wonderful present: a Konica camera with a really good lens and a separate flash unit. After that, I looked forward to having a better time at future opening nights because I could get some good pictures!

Unfortunately, while we were in Chicago, Jackie ended up in the hospital, and he had to undergo triple-bypass surgery. The show, of course, would not go on without him. His illness didn't just end my backstage photography for the time being; it ended the whole tour. Within three days of his operation, the rest of the cast members were heading back to New York. It was the end of the tour, the end of opening nights, and thoughts of another Broadway opening were squelched. I would love to have opened with The Great One on the Great White Way, but it was destined not to be.

The *Sly Fox* experience lasted five months instead of a possible two years, but it was extremely interesting, and quite wonderful. As with so many shows, I came away with some very good friends: actress/writer Catherine Schreiber; actor/singer Jack Landron; and actor/teacher Sandy Morris—people I have kept in touch with over the years, sometimes not seeing them for long periods, but always with a very warm feeling when we do spend time together.

Once I got back to New York, I started running around the city with my new camera, taking lots of pictures, and going back to my boyfriend's place to use his darkroom. I tried to get the technique from reading books on it or asking Bob, but that wasn't very satisfactory. I needed some formal training. Eventually, I began to study darkroom technique at a school, and I finally mastered the basics. So while it was true that I was back to Go in the theatre's version of the game of Life, I also was at the starting point of a hobby that would ultimately lead to a second career.

Carousel

Alan Coleridge, a good friend whom I met through my longtime friend Fiddle (you'll remember her from *The Beauty Part*) called me one day about an upcoming production. Alan was a casting director, but he wasn't working on this particular show; however, he was in the inner circle with many of the production people. He knew that they were still looking for an actress for the part of Mrs. Mullin in a summer tour of *Carousel*. He said he had told the producers about me, and they said that I should call. It was a first-class, top-notch tour, but I said I wasn't really a singer so I felt there was no point in my calling. He responded that it was a non-singing part. I thanked him but didn't follow up on it because I figured a "straight" part couldn't be much of a role since it was a musical. (I guess I'd forgotten about my part in *Sweet Charity*—Ursula was a very good *non*-singing role.)

In any event, about a week later, Alan followed up and asked why I hadn't called the *Carousel* management. I explained my reasoning, and he attempted to convince me that contrary to my assumption, it is an excellent role. I then read Ferenc Molnar's *Liliom,* which *Carousel* is based upon, and I discovered that Mrs. Mullin is actually a good dramatic role. So I made the call and an audition was arranged with the director, James Hammerstein, son of composer Oscar Hammerstein II. (Oscar wrote the book and lyrics to *Carousel;* the music is by Richard Rodgers.) The reading went well; I joined the cast; and within the week, we started rehearsals in New York. It was a Lee Guber-Shelly Gross summer package. (A theatre "package" is a term used to describe a show that has been produced to travel to many theatres, usually on a weekly basis. This is different than a production mounted for a specific theatre, which might later tour. Many packages are "bus & truck" tours, but the ones with star attractions usually travel first class—by air.) Guber-Gross were the biggest producers of summer road shows at the time and always put together a very good production, usually featuring a big-name star.

We had a two-week rehearsal period with almost everyone showing up in the first week except the star of the show. We got most of the play blocked without him and I had a wonderful carefree week with, among others, Susan Bigelow,

Harry Danner, Nancy Eaton, Kevin O'Connor, and Leslie Ann Ray. In week two, Robert Goulet joined us, along with three of his regular back-up singers, who became part of the chorus. When Goulet walked into rehearsals, we were all a bit surprised that he wasn't as tall as we'd expected him to be. Even our director had a six-foot-image of Goulet, so he had cast tall actresses in the four leading lady roles. We were all between 5'8" and 5'10", which means that with heels, we'd all be about six feet tall. Designer Gail Cooper-Hecht immediately got to work and changed our heeled boots to ballet slippers. I then learned the importance of the S curve: You put your ribcage left, and your hips go right, then you do the hokey-pokey…no, no, no, forget the dance. It's just that with your body twisted that way, you can lose an inch or two in height. That did it! It brought us eyeball to eyeball, which worked well.

My scenes were scattered throughout the play and I had a lot of spare time during rehearsals, so I brought my new, good camera to rehearsals and started snapping away. At night I would go home and develop the film. I'd have dinner and then go into my darkroom and start printing. Printing is fun, but time flies in the darkroom. Every evening, after what seemed a very short time, I'd look up and it would be past midnight. As I had to be at the rehearsal hall by 10 a.m., I usually shut down and went to bed. At the next day's rehearsal, I'd bring in the prints I had made and I'd pass them around. There were never batches of different pictures, because I, being a perfectionist, might work on one negative half the night, just to get it right. Using computers, we can do photography work a lot faster today, but I still feel there's nothing like the hands-on time spent in a darkroom.

I was going to rehearsals every day as an actress but my photos—and people's reactions to them—were becoming as important as my role and the acting notes from the director. This *Carousel* actually provided a small but pivotal spin in another career. Not that I had that thought at the moment. I was just having fun with my hobby.

During this period, I got my first order for a headshot. Our director, Jamie, who sported a short beard, said that his agent wanted a new photo of him. The one he was using was outdated since his beard in the picture was long and full, and his headshot was no longer a good representation of him. He wanted to pay me, but I insisted on doing it as a favor. He was stronger in his insistence, and so I got my first paying job as a photographer. I certainly didn't think of myself as a professional at that point, but it was a good feeling to get paid for something I was enjoying so much. I was thrilled when my photo was used, not in the "give-away" playbill, but in the big souvenir program (the one that is *sold* in the lobby of the theatre) and it made quite a hit. The show's conductor, Milton Rosen-stock, saw it, and he wanted a new photo, too. I shot Milton's picture, and I could have done any number of headshots after that, but it wasn't an area I wanted to concentrate on, so I was very selective about saying yes to a request. I had developed a love for photography at that point, but headshots were not my favorite subject. I was more interested in crawling in the grass for a good shot of a flower, climbing over a fence for a closer look at a tree, aiming my camera up, down, and all around, taking odd shots, and beautiful ones, too, but not just posed pictures.

Carousel starts with the Prologue-Waltz Suite: "Carousel." It's almost a ballet and establishes all the characters in an amusement park during the late nineteenth century on the coast of Maine. Mrs. Mullin (my character) is the carousel owner, and Billy Bigelow, played by Goulet, is the arrogant, without-aim-or-ambition, carnival barker, and my employee. He's also my lover. All the girls are attracted to him, and I'm very jealous of everyone he flirts with. In the opening scene, I catch him with two of the youngest and prettiest girls, and we quarrel. I'm constantly firing him and then taking him back, and this time he storms off after the girls. The storyline then follows his romance with Julie Jordan (played by Leslie Ann Ray, followed by Jo Ann Cunningham) and Billy's struggle and ultimate triumph over his character flaws. It's a beguiling story and features some of the most beautiful songs ever written for the musical stage, including "If I Loved You" and "You'll Never Walk Alone." When you hear the score, you can understand why, out of all the shows they created, *Carousel* was Rodgers' and Hammerstein's favorite. Everyone seems to love *Carousel*, including the critics who reviewed our production:

"*Carousel* is a beauty…with a supporting cast that comes up to expectations in every case.…The production is mounted with taste and imagination.…The combination of words and music, book and score is among the most felicitous in the entire Rodgers and Hammerstein collection, including *Oklahoma, South Pacific*, and *The King and I*."—Corbin Patrick, *The Indianapolis Star*

"This classic show [is] one of the most admired and beloved in the American theatre. Harry Danner is a strong-voiced sympathetic Mr. Snow and Robert Darnell, an engagingly villainous Jigger. Jo Ann Cunningham [as Julie] sings nicely and has a delightful smile. Other assets are Nancy Eaton as Nettie Fowler, Marie Wallace as Mrs. Mullin, [and] Jerome Collamore as a very winning Starkeeper."—Bruce Eggler, *The States-Item*

Our tour included a number of interesting cities. We started by playing in the "round" in Long Island and Pennsylvania. We then switched to proscenium stages starting in Indianapolis, and moving on to Atlanta, St. Louis, Miami, Orlando, New Orleans, and ending in Wolf Trap, Virginia.

All through the tour I continued to photograph, and as I got serious about the work, I mostly used black-and-white film. I was drawn to landscapes, flowers, and architecture. I also continued to photograph people, but more candid work than posed. I enjoyed shooting those who weren't aware of what I was doing. I found it more interesting to capture unguarded moments because that's when you capture the soul of a person, not their public persona. It's a little like the actor's approach to a part—we're constantly observing people, seeing what they're really like, what makes them tick.

When we were in Miami, I decided I wanted to get a good sunrise shot, but the first three mornings I tried, I was too late, even though I got up earlier and earlier each day. There's a small window of time, minutes before the sun makes its full appearance, when the sky is perfect, but I kept missing it. At this point, I had become good buddies with Nancy Eaton (she played cousin Nettie—glorious voice, lovely lady, great traveling companion). She agreed to get up with me at 4:30 the next morning and go out on the beach searching for a sunrise. (I wasn't comfortable about going out alone so early.) When I woke up, I saw what I thought was the start of the sun peeking over the horizon. I threw my clothes on, grabbed the loaded camera, and banged on Nancy's door. We raced to the lobby and out onto the beach. It was still pitch black, but I was sure that sun would rise any minute and light up the sky.

After tripping over a few couples necking on the beach, I discovered that my "sun" was really the light on a cruise ship anchored out at sea. We decided to go back to our rooms and come back out in a half-hour, but I didn't wake up again until 8 a.m., so that morning was a bust. I finally got my shot the next morning and rushed it to a lab. What a disappointment when I picked the photos up on our last day in Miami. I had gotten so used to shooting in black-and-white that I didn't even think about the effects of a sunrise without color. Duh! That was another of a long list of lessons I learned as I went along on my photographic journey.

Nancy and I enjoy being tourists, so we took full advantage of our days off, and often spent the day sightseeing, sometimes ending up at a local zoo. One of our most enjoyable days was in St. Louis, when we arranged to meet my friend Nancy Reardon, who was playing Ophelia in *Hamlet* at Missouri Rep in Kansas City. We all went to the zoo/animal park in Forest Park, and enjoyed it so much that we voted it the best zoo we'd ever visited. We then had a great dinner in town, and Nancy R. went back to her theatre the next morning. My only regret was that I wasn't able to see Nancy as Ophelia, but our on-stage schedules were the same, and within the week, we were off to our next city.

The *Carousel* tour ended at Wolf Trap Foundation for the Performing Arts and then we returned to New York, and I think we were all happy to get back after eight weeks on the road. Tours like that are fun but very tiring. We always traveled on our day off, and there were often delays at the airport, lost luggage, and problems checking into hotels.

We had several different types of Equity contracts, a Production Contract—eight performances in six days, and an Outdoor Theatre Contract—one performance a day for seven days, according to the type of theatre we played. During the weeks when we played at out-door theatres, we didn't even have a few hours off. We traveled early Monday morning, arrived in the afternoon and were taken directly to the theatre for rehearsals. Our opening was scheduled for that same night! Sometimes, we didn't even check into the hotel until *after* that first performance.

The saving grace was having wonderful actors in the ensemble, who were also terrific people. I stayed true to form, and established another life-long friendship, this time with Nancy Eaton. We've continued to be great traveling companions, journeying to Ireland, Florence, Rome, and other far-off places, and we're constantly planning new adventures. Friendships like this have become as important to me as my career.

The long summer tour was over, and auditions were starting up again for the fall season. But I wasn't thinking of auditions; I was content with the thought that I was scheduled to go back to Florida in October to play Mabel in George Abbott's *Three Men on a Horse*. The producer, Robert Kantor from the Coconut Grove Playhouse, had contacted me during our week in Miami, and we had made the arrangements for the new production at that time. I was very content. I had just finished a long ten weeks of work, and had six or eight weeks to "play" in the city before my next engagement.

Co-stars:
With Larry Storch;
in *Arsenic and
Old Lace* with
Mary Lucy Bivins;
and with Lee Horsley

Last Licks

New York is great in the fall—my favorite season. It was especially wonderful after doing the long *Carousel* tour, and because I was already signed for the Florida gig in late October, I could just relax and enjoy the city. So I settled back and got more involved in photography, still thinking of it as not much more than a serious hobby.

I set up the darkroom in my apartment and continued to work with black-and-white film. I'd roam around the city with my camera, mostly in Central Park, and shoot whatever caught my eye. Then I'd come home and develop the film, print a contact sheet, and if there were anything good on it, I'd make some prints. I used my kitchen as a darkroom: I had the printer on a wheeled table that had two shelves, and my dodging and burning tools were kept on that. I stored it in my den, and would wheel it into the kitchen to set up shop. My photographic papers were stored in the kitchen cabinets, and all the chemicals were stored under the sink. I had a long counter in the kitchen, originally built to my specifications (height and length) for cooking. But with a plastic shower curtain spread over it, it became the repository for all my trays—developer, stop bath, fixer. When fixing is complete, the print goes in to the water, and that, of course, meant in my kitchen sink. My refrigerator was conveniently placed against the sink, so I could "squeegee" my prints dry. After the squeegee step, I'd go back to the den and lay out all the photos on sheets I had spread across the floor. Sometimes, if I printed a number of photos, the entire living room floor was filled with prints. It made it a little inconvenient when friends or family dropped by, but we managed.

Much like the way those prints were taking over my apartment, photography was taking on greater importance in my life. That's where my interest was for the moment, so when I got a call from my agent to be the standby in a new Broadway play, *Last Licks*, I wasn't sure I wanted to do that. If the opportunity had been to play the main part, I wouldn't have hesitated. On the plus side, it was to be a Shubert Organization production (they were the biggest producers on Broadway, I had already worked for them in *Sly Fox*, and I knew they'd be doing hundreds more Broadway plays), and the writer was Frank Gilroy (the 1965

Pulitzer Prize winner for *The Subject Was Roses).* The director was Tom Conti (earlier in the year he had won the Tony Award for Best Actor in *Whose Life is it Anyway?),* and the star was Ed Flanders, who had won the 1974 Tony Award as Best Actor in *A Moon for the Misbegotten.* It was an exciting group, but I still thought I wanted to honor my commitment in Florida. Then Conti called me and somehow convinced me to accept the *Last Licks* offer. I wanted to do both things but I had to make a choice, and Broadway won out. I prefer to play a role as opposed to being a standby, but I figured it'd give me a chance to watch some really talented people at work and to take pictures backstage. And that's just what I did.

It's a three-character play, about the guilts and hypocrisies between a father (Flanders) and son (J. T. Walsh). The father has been grieving for his "beloved" wife of thirty-nine years, and is resisting his son's efforts to hire a housekeeper. We find out that he wasn't such a great husband when she was alive, hanging out at bars, hitting her occasionally, and often not coming home for dinner. He admits to these things but insists that there had never been any extracurricular sex. When the father finally agrees to a housekeeper, Fiona Raymond (played by Susan Kellerman) appears, and we discover that she has been the father's mistress for a large portion of his married life. She also happens to be a former nun. The story takes off from there.

I watched the rehearsals every day and Conti was an interesting director to observe. He gave each actor the freedom to develop his character, only stopping one if he got out of style with the others. In the meantime, I was taking shots here and there, unobtrusively, because I certainly didn't want to interrupt the process. At night, I went home and straight to my darkroom. There, I would work on the film I shot that day—unless I joined the group at Barrymore's or Charlie's, the local theatrical hangouts. Those evenings were always wonderful, with other actor friends dropping by, and lots of long, heated discussions and show-biz stories.

We rehearsed in late October, into November, and then did ten previews at the Longacre Theatre, and opened on November 20, 1979. There was talk that the three understudies would do a Sunday performance but, unfortunately, the reviews weren't too good and we only had fourteen more performances after that, closing on December 1. Standbys mostly watch rehearsals and take notes, and don't get a chance to rehearse until *after* the play opens. Those post-opening rehearsals are usually not with the director (the stage manager conducts them) and it's with all the other standbys, not with the stars. So unless we had a few more weeks to polish it up, we weren't anxious to get on stage.

Before Tom Conti went back to Britain, he wrote a note to the public that was published by the *New York Times*:

"Occasionally, thank God infrequently, a dreadful error is made by the people who review plays. This has happened with *Last Licks,* and I feel honor-bound for the author, the actors, and the public to say so. Frank Gilroy's play is not a momentous drama about a dreadfully deformed man or a quadriplegic. Nor is it an opera about a psychopathic hairdresser. It is about something much more complex, yet closer to us all—the family.... There are two simple questions I ask myself to assess an audience's enjoyment: Is there intensity in the laughter, and do the silences match that intensity? In the performances of *Last Licks,* the answer was yes in both cases."

I agreed with Tom and was very sorry that the production ended so abruptly. All three actors in the play were delightful people and excellent actors. It would've been interesting to see their characters continue to develop on stage, and fun to get to know them better. But it all ended, and the actors flew home to California, Conti went to London, and I went back to strolling through Central Park for photo opportunities.

On the Road Again

New York is my permanent address, but many times over the years I've been away from it at a moment's notice. A call from my agent would lead to an audition, and before I knew it, I was on the road again. More often than not, it wasn't a tour as were *Carousel* and *Sly Fox*. Usually, the show was at one theatre, in one town, which is considerably easier than touring around the country. That was the case with *Mummer's End*. I'm always happy on my way to an acting assignment and I was doubly happy to get away from the city because I had just broken up with a boyfriend, and a change of pace was welcomed.

It was exciting to be heading for the Folger Theatre in Washington, D.C., since I'd never visited the Capitol. It was January 1977, and within a few weeks of our arrival the inauguration of Jimmy Carter was to take place. (I'd always watched the inauguration ceremonies on television but now I was going to be right up front—or so I thought.) The weather there was pretty exciting too, if that's how to describe a big snowstorm. Just as soon as we got to D.C., a blizzard dumped mountains of snow on the city. That surprised me and I wasn't quite prepared for it, because somehow if I travel to places below Philadelphia, I think I'm going south—which of course *is* the direction I'm heading, but it's not the warm south of Florida. However, with the addition of a warm pair of boots and some scarves, I was ready for anything.

We had a rehearsal scheduled for the morning of January 20, but we convinced our producer/director, Louis Scheeder, to give us some time off, and we all went over to the East Front of the Capitol to watch the inauguration. Well, we didn't get that close; we probably would have seen more on TV, but it was thrilling to be present at (or at least near) such a momentous occasion.

Jack Gilhooley's *Mummer's End* is a comedy about traditions and how they affect four generations of an American family, the O'Rourkes. The tradition they are part of is the highly stylized Philadelphia Mummer's Day Parade—it's the center of their lives. (In real life, there have been Mummer's Clubs since the 1840s with the first formal Mummer's parade staged on January 1, 1901, with prizes for the best-dressed groups.) At first, only men marched in the parade, and even today, women are not officially allowed to march, but sometimes they sneak in, and some men impersonate women. However, originally women did all the work beforehand, designing and sewing their glorious and outrageous costumes. My character, Peaches O'Rourke, begins to rebel against the exclusion of women in the parade, and it's the family's first taste of women's liberation. All of Gilhooley's characters are interesting and funny, and my character was especially delightful to play. I loved that the playwright was at rehearsals every day, openly discussing the characters and the play with the actors and director. That's the beauty of working on a new play at a regional theatre: Everyone is receptive to change, as opposed to on Broadway, where time is limited and so much money is riding on the production. As is typical with regional theatre contracts, we rehearsed for three-and-a-half weeks and played for four weeks. Again, we had fine actors from New York and D.C.—John LaGioia, Mary Carney, Jean Barker, Fred Warriner, Joseph Sullivan, Anne Stone, and John Gilliss. True to form, I gained another good friend, John LaGioia, and he remains so to this day. Once we opened, I became the true tourist once again, and visited the museums, the U.S. Capitol, Lincoln Memorial, the Library of Congress, Georgetown, and any other place I could fit in. Eight weeks go very fast when you're acting at night and running around town all day, and before I knew it, it was time to pack up and go back to New York. It was another short but sweet experience.

After I was back in New York for a while, I auditioned for a new play and got the part of Fuzzy Delgato in John Ford Noonan's *Listen to the Lions*. That was a very interesting play with outrageous characters. My part was a gal who "does shaving cream commercials and yearns for a career in feature films but would settle for getting a prominent obituary." At least that's how she describes herself, or perhaps I should say how playwright Noonan describes her. He's a very talented writer and has a wild, sometimes, surrealistic imagination. It's a hilarious play. We rehearsed and played in Vermont as a joint project of the Performing Arts of Middlebury College, Vermont, with the Aspen Playwrights Conference. They're devoted to the encouragement of American playwrights and the development of American plays. In Vermont, we had rehearsal conditions free from commercial demands, with the playwright constantly revising the play through his collaboration with the company and the critic-in-residence. And that was so stimulating because it was Harold Clurman, the famous writer/director I had studied with back in the sixties. It was the last theatrical venture that Clurman was involved in before his death, and I was happy to be a part of it. He had cancer at the time but one would've never known it. He was a little thinner than usual, but he was as dapper as ever, usually decked out in a black velvet suit. After one of our performances, he was on stage, talking enthusiastically about the play and theatre, and looking like a gentle bear. He said something I've never forgotten, "Some people say I have a passion for the theatre. That's not true. I have a passion for Life!" He passed that passion on to all those around him. To make the experience even better, we had a wonderful cast including Scotty Bloch, Tom Noonan, and Susan Sarandon. Susan had just finished Louis Malle's latest film, *Atlantic City*, written by John Guare, and she threw herself into the work. She was a very free spirit and was great on stage.

There were a number of good Equity Dinner Theatres in the seventies and eighties, and they presented comedies and musicals. Many of the theatres that I played back then have since become Non-Equity houses, which is a pity because it has taken away so much work from the professional actor. On top of that, the ones that are left only do musicals, not straight plays. The first one I appeared at was actually back in the sixties with Fannie Flagg, and after that, I didn't do another one until the seventies. And then I worked at a number of them in the late seventies through the eighties. Three of the productions that I starred in stand out in my memory. Interestingly enough, the same man, Jerry Grayson, directed all three of them. I first auditioned for him in New York for the part of Ann Stanley in *Forty Carats*. We clicked at the first meeting and he told me, right then and there, that he'd like me to play the part. It was to be at the Country Dinner Playhouse in Englewood, Colorado, a suburb of Denver. In many dinner theatres, in a contemporary play, the actor in the starring role provides her own costumes. (I always liked it that way, because most small theatres don't have big budgets for costumes, and they often alter clothes that other actors have worn in previous productions. They never quite fit the body like your own clothes.) *Forty Carats* had a huge costume list. There were ten head-to-toe changes, running the gamut, starting with vacation clothes while my character was on a Greek island, to office attire, to party gowns. One of the questions Jerry asked back at the audition was if I had all those clothes, and my answering "yes" may have been as good a reason as any for hiring me. (He no doubt also thought I was most suited for the role.) In any event, I landed the part and was very pleased about it.

Dinner theatre productions typically have barely a week's rehearsal, so I started studying the script immediately since I was scheduled to leave for Denver the following week. I had five huge suitcases because I also had to have a few clothes for my personal use during the six weeks I would spend in Denver. I was picked up at the airport and driven to a hotel where I stayed until we opened, and then I moved into an apartment. I enjoy staying in a hotel during rehearsals because it's such an intense period, and hotel living is a carefree situation—everything's taken care of for you. You don't even have to make your bed! On the other hand, once the play opens, it's extremely pleasant to have an apartment with all the comforts of home—simple things like your own refrigerator, stove, and toaster.

On the night of my arrival, I went to see the current production at the Playhouse, which was *My Fair Lady*, and met Jerry's (the director) fiancé, who was playing Eliza Doolittle (he had also directed it). They got married on her closing night; she left in the morning for the next theatre on her tour, and he stayed with us to prepare *Carats* for the opening. Theirs was a real show-biz affair.

On the first day of rehearsals, the cast gathered together and I met the seven actors, who were from Denver, Salt Lake City, Chicago, and New York—Michael Tartel, Coleman Creel, Virginia Seymore, Susan-Joan Stefan, Jane Fleming, and Lee Horsley. Lee and I had a good rapport on stage. Off-stage, it was just as good. We became very close and I convinced him to move to New York after we closed, to pursue his career. I introduced him to my agent, Jeff Hunter, who signed him up immediately. Jeff worked very hard for him and really put him on the map. He is perhaps best known for starring in the 1980s detective series *Matt Houston*.

Back to rehearsals—Jerry Grayson was a wonderful director (now he's mostly acting, doing loads of movies, and appearing in many roles on TV in shows like *NYPD Blue*, *The Sopranos*, and *Law & Order*. I'm glad he's having such a busy career as an actor, but I do miss him as a director). It's no small feat to put together a full-length show in one week and do it well, but he knew how to accomplish that, and to have fun in the process.

Playing this role was a real physical workout for me. The stage was in the round with three separate entrances down the aisles. I often would leave one scene by walking up an aisle to the lobby, racing to another entrance on the other side, pulling off my costume in the process. I'd meet the dresser at the top of the new aisle, throw on the next costume, look quickly in a mirror for a last-second adjustment, and coolly make my entrance down the aisle and on stage. Once I almost knocked down an old man in the lobby as he was shuffling his way to the men's room. I may not have physically thrown him off his feet, but the sight of me in my underwear flying past him could have finished him off!

A couple of years later, Jerry was once again directing *Forty Carats*, this time down in Florida, and he invited me to do it there. But that, and my third play with him, comes a bit later.

When I finished the run of my first *Carats*, instead of going straight back to New York, I took a side trip to L.A. I visited with my friends Barbara London and Ruth Buzzi, and I even popped in to see a few casting directors I had known from New York. It was my first introduction to California and it made a good impression on me. But I was living out of a suitcase at that point and I was ready to get back to New York and to wherever destiny or chance would lead me.

East Meets West

It's an age-old question many actors face: "Could I be bi-coastal?" I decided to find out by moving to the West Coast in the early eighties. But if I was going to live on that coast for any length of time, I had to drive. I had gotten a driver's license in New York while I was married, but I only got behind the wheel occasionally after that because Greg did most of the driving. After he died, I used the car for a while but it wasn't as convenient as when Greg simply dropped me off on the way to his office. Alone, it became complicated. I had to find a parking spot or an available garage once I got to my destination—no easy feat in Manhattan. Mostly, the car sat in the garage around the corner from my apartment, so I finally sold it to my *Somerset* co-star Ed Winters. (The characters we portrayed, India and Chuck, never got along, but Ed and I were good friends.) So the big, baaad, black Cadillac was out of my life. I always connected black Cadillacs with Greg since that's all he ever drove, trading an old one in for the newest model every few years, and it was tough to make the decision to sell. But once I did, I was glad that I let it go. An era had come to a close.

At the point when my psyche was ready to try L.A., I hadn't been in the driver's seat for nine years, and I was apprehensive about driving again. So I took a bunch of lessons in New York; going onto highways, into tunnels, and over bridges, until I felt confident I could handle the traffic. I then packed nine suitcases, and on September 9 (I like the number nine) flew to La La Land, giving myself two years to experience it. I kept my apartment in New York and came back to the city many times because my mother was experiencing health problems, and I wanted to see her regularly.

When I arrived in L.A., I stayed with my good friends Cherry and Steven Katz. (Cherry was the pitcher on many of my Broadway Show League softball teams while I was playing first base.) Cherry drove us around to apartment-hunt, and I found the perfect place, fully furnished, at Toluca Lake's Oakwood Garden Apartments on Barham Boulevard. The apartment had a small balcony overlooking the foot of the Hollywood Hills, and the complex had all the amenities I could wish for—tennis courts, swimming pools, and small gyms; and it was centrally located (near most of the studios). It turned out to be a great choice.

As soon as my living quarters were settled, I rented a car. After a while, I realized that a lot of money would go down the drain on rental fees. Why not buy a car? I hunted around and finally bought a white hatchback Toyota. I was thrilled with that car. Even though Greg and I owned the Cadillac, a much bigger, prettier car than this little one, the Toyota was all mine and I felt like a kid again. I experienced the same youthful feeling about my profession because I had to start all over; setting up appointments, seeing agents and casting directors, and figuring out any other contacts I might have. It was the game of Life once more. You go so far and feel like you're on top of the world, and one day you wake up and you're back to Go—meaning, "Start all over again." And like most games, it was constantly challenging, occasionally frustrating, and often fun.

Many commercials, soap operas, and other TV shows had originated in New York over the years, but those productions slowly moved out to L.A., and that was the game I wanted to be involved in. Very early on, I signed with a commercial agent, got new pictures, and started going out on auditions. My first one was in a Santa Monica studio. I picked up the script in the morning, drove over to the beach and sat on the boardwalk steps studying the scenes for my afternoon audition. It was a delightful way to read a script. I landed my first L.A. job, which was a part in an industrial film (a promotional or sales film for a specific industry) to be shot in San Pedro.

It was to be filmed in an old courthouse, and the actors had to report in at 6 a.m. I wanted to make sure that I arrived on time, so I did a test-run a few days before—all city streets, not freeways. I always called AAA beforehand and got explicit directions to and from my new destination. (These days, I'd use Map Quest on the Internet or have a navigation gadget in my car.) I treated driving as if it were a course I was taking in school. At first, I just drove on streets, even maneuvering so that I only had to make right turns in traffic during the initial weeks. When I felt secure, I promoted myself to crossing canyons, and graduated to freeways. At least that was my plan. But my preview trip to San Pedro sped things up a bit. I arrived in town, explored it and found the location for the shoot, ate at a local restaurant and within a few hours headed back. Somehow I accidentally took a road that led right onto a freeway. Once I was on it, I just kept going. It was a good first run, because it was Thanksgiving eve and the freeway was jammed. All the cars went at a leisurely pace, and I have no doubt that I was the only driver pleased with the traffic jams.

Living at the Oakwood Garden Apartments was a terrific experience. In addition to its convenient location, the facilities allowed me to play tennis and swim, and workout at the gym. But best of all was the large outdoor Jacuzzi. At around

7 p.m. each day, it became a great meeting place for old and new show-biz friends, since a large number of actors lived in the complex. One day I met an actor in the parking area outside of Building M—*my* building (they were designated A to Z). After a short conversation, I found out that he lived in the two-bedroom apartment above me, and his roommate was Michael Stroka (Aristede from *Dark Shadows*). I only had a working relationship with him during the filming of *Dark Shadows* and we never saw each other outside the studio, but I wanted to see him immediately. We all met for drinks that night, and that was the start of a wonderful friendship with Mike.

Oakwood was undeniably the place to renew old friendships. One morning, after my gym workout, I walked into the sales office to pay my rent and bumped into John Vari (Hampton Playhouse producer/actor). It turned out that he was living in the same apartment complex but in another building. He often went to L.A. in September for pilot season, after the Hampton theatre season ended. Over the twelve years since I'd appeared at the Playhouse, I attended parties he and Al Christie (Playhouse producer/director) had given in New York, but we didn't run around together. In L.A., we had a chance to go to dinner and develop our friendship. One evening, he invited me back to the Playhouse to be resident leading lady in his upcoming season. I grabbed at the opportunity. Seems like an odd road to take (New Hampshire by way of California), especially since my intention was to do television work that year. However, I remembered all those delicious summers of the past in Hampton, and accepted with pleasure.

The opening show was to be Neil Simon's *I Ought to Be in Pictures* starring Larry Storch as my boyfriend. Larry's television, theatre, film, and nightclub credits run a mile long, and we all remember him fondly as Corporal Agarn in ABC's *F Troop*. Larry also lived in L.A. in the eighties and so did Carol Newell, the actress playing his daughter, so we arranged to have some pre-rehearsal meetings and read-throughs of the script to get a jump-start on the work. Carol and I would drive up to his Hollywood Hills home, and we'd leisurely read the play. Larry's wife, Norma, was great—acting as our stage manager, prompter, and supporter. These informal get-togethers also gave us a chance to get to know each other very well.

I met new casting directors, appeared in some commercials and another industrial, and explored L.A. with my old and new friends. Before I knew it, the month of June arrived and I made arrangements to go back east for the summer. I closed up my California apartment, put my car in storage, promised myself that I'd come back to L.A. at the end of the summer, and happily took off. Everything went very fast and next thing I knew, I had moved into a huge Hampton house with a few other actors, had rented a bike for the summer, and had my four scripts ready to go. In my early days at Hampton, there were ten shows scheduled for the summer, one a week. Most of the summers that I went there, I did three shows in a row, which was very manageable. Many of the other actors were there as *resident* actors, and played in practically every one of the season's ten shows. An exhausting thought! By the time I returned in '81, they were doing each production for two-week periods, which made it much more achievable. That should add up to five plays for me, but the beauty part was that I wouldn't be in the third play and that eased my schedule considerably.

And it was a great summer. We opened with the Simon play and it was a highlight of the season. During the rehearsals, Larry, Norma, Carol, and I got on famously. We would drive to local restaurants or to Portsmouth and spend wonderful evenings together, eating lobsters and other rich New England food. Larry always had us laughing throughout our dinners. He can do imitations of anyone and they're always so funny. The waiters never knew what to make of us—sometimes Larry would introduce the three of us as, "My daughter, my girlfriend, and my wife." While we were hysterically laughing, he'd top it all with another funny quip. He also referred to us as "The Fearsome Foursome," and to this day he will still greet me with that phrase. He and Norma were the most generous friends I've ever known, and we had a ball together. The work on stage—which, after all, is what I was there for—was equally good.

During the run of *I Ought to Be in Pictures,* we started rehearsals for Bernard Slade's *Romantic Comedy,* and opened two weeks later. I acted alongside Kevin Tighe in the second play, and he was also wonderful to work with. Kevin is an L.A.-born actor, who came to fame with his portrayal of paramedic Roy DeSoto in the popular TV series *Emergency,* and has continued his TV career through the years. (He's also the father of actress Jennifer Tighe.) This was a return engagement for Kevin, and the audiences were pleased to have him back.

Between the second play and the fourth, I had a few days off, since I wasn't scheduled to appear in *I Love My Wife.* I took a quick trip down to New York to see my mother and a few friends, and I experienced the difference between a big city and a small town. When I arrived in Hampton, after a twelve-year absence, I went around to all the shops I knew from past years, and they were all there, in the same spots, with the same people behind the counters. The four or five restaurants that were there in '69 were also still operating, along with two new ones. Otherwise, *everything* was the same. Quite the contrary when I visited the big city after five weeks of being away. I went to 79th Street and Columbus Avenue to meet a date at Gleason's Public House Restaurant, and it was gone! In its place was a three-story-deep excavation, and construction of a skyscraper had already begun. Well, since I love change, and my permanent home is New York, I guess I live in the right place.

Within a few days, I was back in Hampton and in rehearsals for the big musical of the season, *Burlesque Scandals of 1981*. After the Playhouse's first production of the play *Burlesque*, audiences began to request it for future seasons. In fact, it turned into the most requested show, and every two or three years there was another version of it. Back in the sixties, I had appeared twice in the straight play *Burlesque,* to which musical numbers had been added, and I played the part of a stripper named Bonny. But by the late seventies and eighties, they were using real strippers, with old corny burlesque skits, and song-and-dance numbers. The '81 version was completely new, conceived by John Vari and Emil Sanzari. I played the comedienne and did many of the comedy skits, which I adored, especially since I worked with Frank O'Brien, Frank Vohs, and Richard Kennedy, all wonderful comic actors. Their comic genius truly added to the hilarity of the performances.

Myra Bruhl was my character in the final play that summer, Ira Levin's *Deathtrap*, a tongue-in-cheek whodunit for which Kevin Tighe returned to play my husband, Sidney. Another husband who killed me! (This was getting repetitious.) Actually, he simply scared me to death; I had a fatal heart attack. Ken Olin, who had just started working in television, played the college student, Clifford Anderson, in our production. Immediately after Hampton, his career took off with parts on the series *Falcon Crest, Hill Street Blues,* and *thirtysomething. Deathtrap* turned into a very interesting production, which I enjoyed very much, even though I wasn't wild about lying dead on stage while actors walked and talked above me (shades of *DS*).

It was a wonderful summer of work and play, in a beautiful environment, with the best of people. I have fond memories of the entire summer, and it was over all too soon. But I was also ready to get back to L.A. to try another year in my new home-away-from-home. I went to New York for a week and then flew back to California. At home immediately in my nice little apartment and car, I quickly got back to the business of drumming up some business and resuming my Hollywood life. In this second season, I signed with a TV agent (again through my connection with John Vari—"Thank you, John"). Up to that point, I was strictly working with a commercial agent. My new agent started getting me out to auditions for TV shows, and I soon landed a few.

I co-starred on *Fantasy Island* in an episode called "The Case Against Mr. Roarke/Save Sherlock Holmes." Peter Lawford played Holmes, with Mel Ferrer as Moriarity, and Donald O'Connor as Dr. Watson. I met them all at the studio but didn't have any scenes with them. I had a short and sweet scene with Ricardo Montalban. I played a librarian, which is usually a plain-Jane type of character, but not on *Fantasy Island*. Everyone looked glamorous on that show. It's not that they made me up to look like a femme fatale—far from it. But the costumer told me that all the women's clothes on the show had to be silk, in lovely pastel shades, and the skirts had to be short. I did wear my hair a little plainer than usual as the librarian, Mrs. Vinton, and wore granny glasses to look studious. (Now I wear them so I can read!) We sat around a lot through the day, had one rehearsal, after which the director came to me and whispered in my ear, "You were perfect, do it exactly that way on tape." That worried me for a moment; I wasn't even sure what I had done. I was just testing the waters, trying a few things, thinking we'd rehearse a bit and discuss the character. But I found out that on these episodic shows, even less time is spent rehearsing with the actors than on soaps.

Sitting around talking with *Fantasy*'s star, Ricardo Montalban, was fun. We mostly spoke about New York and he said that figuring out what to wear in New York winters was always a problem because of central heating. When you dressed for the outdoors, it was always so uncomfortable indoors. I agreed with him. He advised wearing summer clothes in the winter and winter clothes in the summer. I never took his advice but often thought of him as I stood in a hot subway car in the middle of winter, dressed in my woolies with sweat pouring down my back. He was a charming gentleman and I enjoyed my short time with him.

My next audition was for *Fame*, the TV series based on the hit movie of the same name. When I walked out of the meeting, I assumed I didn't get the part, because the director never looked at me once during my reading. (I observed that with my peripheral vision.) When I finished, he thanked me and I was on my way. I was surprised when my agent called and said I had the part. I figured later that he liked to *hear* the actor more than *see* her. My character was Mrs. Murphy, mother to Kathy, to be played by Connie Needham. We taped the following week and again, I was amazed to see how little time we spent on the set. I was in the makeup and hair department longer than in rehearsals. And once the scenes were blocked, they called in the "second team," a term I hadn't heard before. The principal actors were obviously the first team. The second team consisted of the stand-ins, who made all the moves for lights and cameras—as in the movies. Because I was used to soap work where the actors did everything for themselves, this seemed strange. However, I'm sure it was a welcome rest to the actors who were playing lead roles every day, every week. It all went smoothly, if uneventfully, and soon I was once more auditioning and discovering L.A.

In the meantime, I continued renewing friendships and reconnecting with my old friends from TV and theatre. Ruth Buzzi and I got to spend time together again, and I met her wonderful husband, Kent. Barbara London (from my *Gypsy* days) and I became really close buddies again, along with her two girls. I loved going to their home, puttering around in the backyard, and photographing their many cats and dogs. Nick Coster and Alice Herson (*Somerset*) and I hooked up again, as I did with Frank Campanella from *Nobody Loves an Albatross*; the list goes on and on—all my actor friends seemed to be living in California. Many were involved with theatre groups there, and I started looking into that, but then I decided that if and when I wanted to do theatre, I'd go back to New York.

I was having fun with photography, so I began photography classes. The teacher, Conrad, at the Women's Village on Sepulveda Boulevard, turned out to be wonderful, and I managed to shoot some prize-winning photos during field trips with him. Two that stand out for me are *L.A. Freeway* (a time exposure of that wild traffic at sunset) and a photo of a Native American woman on horseback atop the Will Rogers Park looking down at smoggy Century City in the background. Her back is to us but you can feel the tears in her eyes. I also won my first photography prize—"First Place in the Black and White Division/People Category" at the Burbank Public Library, for *Reverie*, a photo I had taken prior to going out west. You can read more in "Photography: A New Beginning."

As that second summer was coming to a close, I reevaluated my career goals. After all, it would be two years in September; the amount of time I had given myself to make a choice about where I wanted to live, or to decide if I could live in both places. Commuting back and forth on a regular basis didn't appeal to me, so being bi-coastal was out—it had to be one place or the other. My TV agent of less than a year wanted me to stay put, trying to convince me that it took a couple of years to really get established in Hollywood, but I was restless. I made my decision. On September 9, with even more than nine suitcases, I flew back to my city—to the museums, the concert halls, and the theatres; to walking instead of driving for hours; to Central Park; to my family and friends—to New York, New York…as we all know, it's a helluva town!

Back to New York…or Was I?

New York is truly my town. I'm glad I tried life in L.A. because it made me realize how much I love New York. Even though so many of my friends lived in California, some of my dearest friends and my family were in the city. I got back into the swing of things in the Big Apple, did a few commercials, shot a number of photographs, changed agents (actually, I went back to my first agent, Michael Hartig), and began auditioning for shows. Because as Shakespeare once wrote, "The play's the thing." I was in and out of town after that as there was more work outside New York. When a part intrigued me, I was ready for it, and packed my bags once more, just as long as I could get back to New York at the end of the run.

One of the plays I got cast in was a second production of *Forty Carats*, directed by my friend Jerry Grayson. I was happy to be back working with him. This time it was in St. Petersburg, Florida. Upon my arrival at the airport, the theatre's publicist met me at the luggage carousel as I picked out my five suitcases (and prayed that none went astray). She drove me to the car rental place, got me a beautiful car, then sped off to St. Petersburg Beach in her car, with me behind her in hot pursuit. Just as the management did in Denver, they arranged a hotel room for me during the rehearsal week. This time it was at the beach, and it was a delight. Each afternoon, following rehearsals, I'd take the drive back to the beach, change into a bathing suit, walk along the shore, have a dip in the ocean, come back and shower. Then I'd go out for a good shore dinner, review the blocking and other notes from the day's rehearsal, and go to bed. The only thing I didn't like were the seagulls that came by the hundreds onto my balcony in the morning. If not for the birds, I would have had breakfast out there but instead I went to a beach restaurant and then drove to the theatre for rehearsal. Once we opened, I was given a charming two-bedroom apartment about two blocks from the theatre. But of course, I had my handy car, so I acted like all suburbanites and drove back and forth every day.

Having that extra bedroom was very nice. My sister Dolly came down and spent my birthday with me. (I never do ordinary work on my birthday, since I always like to celebrate, but being in a good play on that special day is the best celebration of all.) My boyfriend of the moment visited, and the work experience turned into another holiday.

When you work on the same play with an entirely new cast, it's a very different experience. I liked the first one better, and it may not be because it really was any better, but just because it was the first. (It reminds me of the unfortunate actor who replaces a popular TV soap actor. Quite often, the audience doesn't like the replacement as much, and invariably the producers fire the new actor and try to rehire the first actor, or get rid of the character altogether.) I did get to know the first cast more intimately, and that makes a difference. Nevertheless, it was a good experience, and being in St. Petersburg was a relaxing tonic.

I vividly remember Uta Hagen's performance in *Who's Afraid of Virginia Woolf?* on Broadway back in the sixties, so when my agent called me to audition for the part of Martha, I knew I was in for a challenging time if I got the part. The play is a powerful work of art and is also very disturbing. It won the 1962-63 Drama Critics Circle Award and the Tony Award, and had been made into a 1966 film with Elizabeth Taylor and Richard Burton.

The audition was for Peter Clough and was to be the third offering in the 1984-85 season at Capital Repertory Company in Albany, New York. Several actors I knew had worked up at Cap Rep and all had been very pleased with the productions there. So I went to the audition well prepared, read a number of scenes for Peter, and got the part. That's when the work began.

Martha was one of the toughest roles I've ever played. I never before had to sit down and memorize a part, but with this play, I did. An act would end, and with any other ordinary playwright, it would probably be the conclusion of the play, but with Albee it was followed by two more acts even more powerful than the last. I was glad I was out of town doing this play, because once we opened, I would sleep late (9 a.m.), go to the gym, have a massage, lunch at a restaurant, go back to my place and nap, and then get up and go through the entire play before I went to the theatre. On Saturday and Sunday, we played four shows back to back (a 4 p.m. matinee and an 8 p.m. show on both days). Sometimes, by Sunday evening, as I was standing in the wings waiting to make an entrance, I'd begin to think I was in the wrong place, that I'd done that scene already, it seemed so fresh in my mind. Then I'd calm down, hear my cue, enter, and hope for the best. The other actors often felt that way too, but somehow we were always in the right place and we'd get through the performance without too many mistakes. It was an exhausting role, and I wouldn't want to do it again. But I was thrilled to have played it, and truly grateful that while I was developing and playing the part, I was away from my hectic life in New York, and could concentrate on only one thing—Martha and *Virginia Woolf.*

For a while, I was going from one regional theatre to another, with commercials in-between while I was in New York, but I didn't have to travel for the next play I landed. The theatre was in Queens, next door to home. The play was *Along Came A Spider*, a new mystery by Robes Kossez, with direction by Sue Lawless. The theatre was on the site of the 1960 World's Fair Grounds, right across from Shea Stadium. World-famous architect Philip Johnson originally designed the building to be an exhibition hall for the New York State Pavilion. This round cement building was converted into a theatre and was the home of The Theater in the Park, which was in its third season.

The acoustics in the building were very tricky, cement being the worst material for conducting sound. In some parts of the theatre, you could hear a pin drop on stage, and in others, no matter how loudly you spoke, you couldn't be heard. Hopefully, we overcame that with a good sound system, but I still made sure that my friends or family didn't sit in certain seats.

Because Queens is just across the East River from Manhattan, cast members didn't have to pack bags and move out of town. Instead, we rehearsed in a large room at the theatre. We were driven out each morning, which, depending on traffic, took us anywhere from a half-hour to an hour. It was a great way of getting to know the other actors: Betsy von Furstenberg, Michael Hirsch, Katherine Elizabeth Neuman, Keith Perry, E. G. Baker, and Betty Low. We finished our limited run and luckily my next play was also in the city.

I was even closer to home this time at the Off-Broadway South Street Theatre on 42nd Street. It was David Rabe's *In the Boom Boom Room,* newly revised, produced by the Orange Theatre Company and directed by Jerrold Brody. I remember the audition being very interesting and most unusual. It was more like being back in Wynn Handman's acting class and doing one of our improvisations. The director asked me to read a scene with the actor Ron August, who was already cast as the husband. He's a very vulnerable and realistic actor, and we played off each other very well. Suddenly we were improvising and jitterbugging together, and the dance got wilder and wilder. At one point, Ron was swinging me around so much that I stumbled and fell. But it was okay, we stayed in character and it just added an extra dimension to our interpretations. I got the part. Within the week, we started rehearsing on the stage of the theatre where we would eventually open. I like that. It helps so much to work in the actual space even though it's without furniture, except for a few hard chairs and tape on the floor to indicate the layout of the room. A rehearsal hall, no matter how accurately they measure it out, never has the same spatial feeling. The only other time I experienced that was with *The Right Honourable Gentleman*, as you read about earlier.

The play is the study of a go-go dancer named Chrissy, as she searches for some meaning in her brutally degrading and humiliating world. I played her mother, who originally wanted to abort her, and who makes no bones about it. Ron was the father who probably had abused her sexually—the head of another dysfunctional family. It's an extremely harsh play, and because we played during the Thanksgiving holiday and pre-Christmas period, audiences weren't too receptive to it. Again, it was planned for a limited run, and when it was over, I was once more out photographing the streets and parks of New York.

In April 1987, a few years after I had done the Florida production of *Forty Carats* for director Jerry Grayson, I got a call from him asking me to audition for a play called *Alone Together*. I did the audition and he cast me in the role of Helene. He then asked me to come back and read with some of the men he was considering for my husband. I read with all of them and then conferred with Jerry, and I was delighted when he agreed with me that Bill Lewis would be the best actor for the part. I could tell from our reading that he would play the part very well, and would also be a great deal of fun to be with.

Within two weeks, we were all on our way to Omaha, Nebraska's Firehouse Dinner Theatre. It was a unique theatre that had once been a firehouse (it still had the sliding pole in one of the dressing rooms, but unfortunately, I didn't get to use it). I liked the setup of that theatre very much because, unlike all the other dinner theatres I was familiar with, this one was separate from the restaurant. Most are set up as restaurants with a small raised platform for the stage (often in the round), and invariably you hear dishes and silverware rattling, people talking to waiters or wandering about freely to go to the bathrooms. Not here. At the Firehouse, the audience members had dinner in a real restaurant, and then they moved to the theatre (no tables, just school-type seats with side trays that lifted up). The one concession they made was that coffee and drinks were served. The drinks were served before the play started, and during intermission, but never during the performance, so it was always very quiet.

The building had a nice bar, and afterward some of the audience and most of the cast would stop in to have a drink or two. Bill always made me laugh—some nights he'd step up to the bar, order a drink, and say to the bartender, "I don't *want* this drink, I *need* this drink." It wasn't true but it was always good for a laugh. We rented a car together, played tennis together, found fun restaurants to go to, and enjoyed Omaha both on stage and off. On a day off, he went back to New York to finalize his divorce and when he came back, one of the actors (who played our youngest son) and I drove to the airport to pick him up—we were like a family. This closeness often happens to the cast of a play (we're holed up together for weeks at a time, focusing on the same goal, and usually spend all our spare time together too), and when it does, it's super. That particular day was my birthday (seems like I often worked on my birthday) and Bill took me to lunch and bought me a bottle of champagne. It wasn't a romance, just a wonderful warm friendship, and we're still good friends to this day.

My favorite production during the eighties was *Barflys, Part I,* a showcase production (meaning no pay), something I hardly ever did. Yet this was a very special piece. Once I read it and met and auditioned for the director, Lou Vuolo, I knew I wanted to be involved in it. The character, Connie Mae, was quite different from anyone I had played in New York, and I liked her right from the beginning. The writing by Fred Crecca was really good, and I knew just from my audition that working on *Barflys, Part I,* and with this director, would be a very positive experience.

And that's the best reason to do a "showcase." I put quote marks around the word because I consider it a misnomer. Most actors accept parts in showcases in order to *show their talents* to agents and casting directors. The problem is that those important people almost never come—not because they're uninterested in the actors, but because there are just too many choices of performers and plays to see, from Broadway to Off-Broadway to Off-Off Broadway to showcases. If they accepted half of the invitations to see showcases, they'd be occupied all day and night, right through the weekends, and have no time to take care of their business, which is to cast the productions they're working with. Having said that, I know they have to keep finding new talent (new to them, at least) and they *will* go to some showcases, but that's just luck and if it happens, it's great. But it shouldn't be the main reason for an actor to get involved in a showcase production.

As for me, I've never wanted to waste my time, so one of *my* good reasons for accepting a showcase is that I love the character in the play. In fact, I've always said that I'd take a part if it answered *yes* to at least one of the following three questions (answering yes to all three is the best of all worlds):

1.   Do I love the part, or at least, really like it?

2.   Will it advance my career?

3.   Will I make lots of, or at least some, money doing it?

In a showcase situation, it's often impossible to answer *yes* to numbers two and three, so the part had better be wonderful. With *Barflys, Part I,* I liked Connie Mae and the play very much. In fact, I loved working on that character—she was so vulnerable and lovable, even though, in the play, she turns everyone away from her. She's an extremely disappointed woman, a sad, lonely, alcoholic, desperately seeking to make a connection with someone, even if just for one night. It's a bittersweet story, very funny, and extremely touching.

It isn't a long piece, so it was presented as a double bill along with another one-act play. It was produced at the Grove Street Playhouse in Greenwich Village, and as with all showcases, it just ran for a limited period. Our union, Actors' Equity, regulates the timing, and only allows a showcase production to run for sixteen performances, which can be spread out over a number of weeks, often playing Fridays through Sundays. So it was almost over before we started, but it was a good fruitful seven weeks (counting rehearsals), and it was one of those experiences that I fondly remember. And as with so many shows, I ended up with a really dear friend, my director, Lou. We've worked on several pieces since then, but mostly it's our friendship that means so much to me.

Lou and I brought a monologue from *Barflys, Part I* to a *Dark Shadows* Festival, and I performed it for the fans. I did it with a costume I had put together, finding items in vintage stores, and making my own hat. The hat was essentially a huge red ribbon that I tied in a bow around my head. I had seen a woman on the bus wearing something like it and thought it would be perfect for Connie Mae, and it was very funny, too. She's a little drunk when the scene starts, so when I was on my way down to the stage, there were a few fans on the elevator, and they tried to engage me in conversation. They know I'm always very friendly, but this time I waved them off and wouldn't talk, since I was preparing for the scene. I also was just leaning against the wall, like I was propped up, and I'm sure some of them thought I had too much Chardonnay. It wasn't until they saw me on stage that they realized it wasn't me they saw on the elevator, but Connie Mae. Again, when I get involved and am fond of a character, she and I often become one. At various times over the years, I've done other performances at Festivals—from more monologues, to a reading of a scene from *MacBeth* with Jonathan Frid, to a sequel to *Dark Shadows* in which about a dozen cast members reunited on stage to bring our characters up to date. (In *Return to Collinwood*, I actually played a new character, since all of mine had met their demises. I played Jessica Loomis, loud-mouthed wife of Willie, reprised by John Karlen.)

During the eighties, I wasn't doing productions in the big Broadway houses where I had first started, but I found that theatre can be very satisfying no matter where you play, as long as you have a good part and are working with talented professionals. Then you can perform anywhere: a barn in New Hampshire, a college auditorium in Georgia, an ol' opera house in Michigan, and even a showcase in an Off-Off Broadway house.

Lion in Winter: Marie with Jonathan Frid and David Moore

The Lion in Winter:
Jonathan Frid
Takes Me To College

Those couple of years I spent working on *Dark Shadows* brought many other positive experiences into my life—and has been a catalyst that helped me meet several people who have become good friends. In 1992, at a *DS* Festival in California, I met a charming actor/director named David Moore, who became an instant friend and with whom I was soon working.

We met at a luncheon hosted by *DS* star Jonathan Frid at the Marriott Hotel. Jonathan had invited me because he wanted me to meet David, who was running the theatre department at Georgia College (in Milledgeville) at that time. David would bring in a guest star and a professional director for certain productions, and Jonathan had appeared on their stage in two of his one-man-shows in 1991 and 1992. David's plan was to produce *The Lion in Winter* during the winter semester in '93 and he had already arranged for Jonathan to direct it. Jonathan felt that it would be a good idea to bring in an Actors' Equity guest star for the role of Eleanor of Aquitaine, and he thought that I would be a good choice for the part. Naturally, it was arranged that I would sit next to David, and we had such a delightful time together that I knew I would enjoy working with him. I still didn't know the exact dates for the production in Georgia, and I hadn't yet been formally asked to do the part, but as soon as I got back to New York, I read the play. I had seen it years before, and knew the part was good, but upon reading it, I changed my opinion to *great* role. As soon as the date for rehearsals was set, David called and offered me the part, and of course I accepted.

About a month before I was to leave for Milledgeville, Jonathan and I took an excursion on the Eighth Avenue subway (the A train) to visit the Cloisters, the medieval branch of the Metropolitan Museum of Art, in Upper Manhattan. It's a beautiful four-acre replica of five medieval French cloisters (quiet places devoted to religious seclusion), and holds approximately five thousand works of art from medieval Europe, with particular emphasis on the period in which *The Lion in*

Winter takes place. It was a dull, dank, dreary day, but as soon as we entered the Cloisters, saw the beautiful paintings and statues, and heard the medieval music, our moods brightened. We really immersed ourselves in those times, and we were delighted to find a stone carving of Eleanor, the real-life inspiration for the character I was studying. Jonathan bought a number of CDs, and some were later used in our production. It was a very enlightening museum visit.

Jonathan flew to Georgia a week earlier than I, to do preliminary work with the actors, and to finish the casting process. Every part in the play is a good one, but some required maturity and a strong acting background. He decided to have Peter Pauze, a teacher at the college and the set designer, play Henry II, King of England. For the powerful role of Richard, he cast David, which delighted me. Richard is the oldest son and Eleanor's favorite (he became my favorite, too). Then there is John, the youngest son and Henry's favorite, and Geoffrey, the middle son and nobody's favorite (meaning the characters, not the actors—all the students were talented and charming). Then there were a few friends of the court; although I'm not sure "friend" is the correct word for the young French Princess, Alias. You see, Alias is King Henry's mistress, and Eleanor is King Henry's wife—not a friendly situation, but very intriguing.

When I arrived at the airport in Atlanta, I was immediately shown that famous southern hospitality. David met me, took me to lunch, showed me around town, and then we drove to Milledgeville. I was taken to my residence, which turned out to be a suite in the old Governor's Mansion (built in 1835). Milledgeville was the capital of Georgia back then, and eight of Georgia's governors lived there consecutively until 1868, and I was to live there for my six-week-stay in Milledgeville. Today, the first two floors of the mansion are a museum and are used for important dinners and other special events for the college. The top floor has been turned into a huge apartment for the president of the college. However, the then-president preferred to live in his own house, so they used part of the mansion for his executive offices, and saved three bedrooms for visiting VIPs (like Jonathan and me). We also shared a living room and a nice kitchen. With its columned entrance, the mansion resembled the Old House from *Dark Shadows*, so Jonathan and I were quite at home. I loved my bedroom and its old four-poster bed, shelves of rare books, a fireplace (Alma, the manager of the mansion, picked fresh camellias and put them on my mantelpiece every day), and a rocking chair—my favorite kind of seat. I remember one night, rocking and studying my script, I was getting dizzy from all the words, and needed a change of pace. I went through the bookcase and pulled down an 1897 almanac. (That was the year that *DS*'s Crazy Jenny lived at Collinwood.) It was fascinating!

Comparing that year with the current one was very interesting reading. It did the trick, and I was able to go back to my script refreshed.

We were treated royally there. Perry Moore, David's father, had just bought a Lincoln Town Car for himself, but he graciously lent it to Jonathan for the entire stay. It only had thirty-nine miles on it when he handed the keys to Jonathan. We drove around town in style before we went home to our elegant mansion. David's family was always helping us out. His mother, Stella, lent me thirteen of her necklaces to use in one of my last prison scenes in the play, when Eleanor is losing her mind from the isolation (she goes through all her jewels, using them as remembrances of her life, putting on one after the other, until she's completely adorned with jewels). The Moores also gave us our closing night party, but first came all those weeks of rehearsal.

A five-week rehearsal period sounds like a great luxury, but because it was a college production, we could only rehearse in the evenings after class—from 7 to 10 p.m. We needed those five weeks and more. Adding up the hours, it's not really that many, and it's a very complex play. At the start of the play, Eleanor has been in captivity for almost ten years. She had tried to wage a war against her husband, King Henry, and of course he didn't care for that, so he had her captured and exiled to the tower of Salisbury. But Henry isn't all bad; he lets Eleanor out occasionally for good behavior, and the action of the play takes place during those times. There's one intrigue upon another in the play and it's quite exciting. It ends with a scene between Henry and Eleanor that goes beyond their anger and struggle and vindictiveness, and you see the great love and respect they have for each other. It's quite emotional.

And we all did our homework; Jonathan and I often worked together in the evenings, polishing the many nuances of my character. David and I also got together every morning, exercising our bodies and minds by speed-walking around the campus, running our lines, and discussing the play. And, most important, we developed a close friendship during that time, one that still flourishes.

It's interesting how the relationship between Jonathan and me developed. We had a good working rapport during the *Shadows* days (after all, at one point, his Barnabas turned my Megan into a vampire), but we never saw each other socially. Our friendship really started at the *Dark Shadows* Festivals in the 1980s, and blossomed when he was preparing and presenting his one-man shows around New York starting in the late eighties. I went to many of them, and they were always followed by a celebratory dinner. After that, even if he weren't doing a show, we'd get together and go out to dinner, often with Louis Edmonds joining us. (Louis was another *DS* actor that I got to know and love in those later years.)

Eleanor was one of the most exciting characters I've ever worked on. She's passionate, vital, domineering, clever, sensual, independent, and *liberated*. Even in the twenty-first century, she would have been ahead of her time, but she lived in the twelfth century. She was the Duchess of Aquitaine, and was in command of as much territory as the King of France. Her grandfather, Duke William IX, who idealized women and established the Court of Love, had composed poetry and songs, and she inherited his talents and carried on the tradition. She could compose a poem, set it to music, play it, and sing it. She grew up with music and great literature and was a champion chess player. She loved chess because of the element of excitement in the conflict, and Eleanor *always* emerged the victor. She surrounded herself with poets and troubadours, all of whom wrote love songs and poems idealizing her. It was the Age of Chivalry and she expected men to have exquisite manners and express themselves with elegance and beauty. She knew what she wanted and never allowed anyone or anything to prevent her from doing what she desired (until Henry came along and threw her in prison). She was quite a woman.

After our evening rehearsals, Jonathan, David, and I usually went to a restaurant for a change of pace and some relaxation. On one occasion, when Jonathan and I arrived back at the mansion, there was a huge, black, chauffeured, Cadillac limousine parked outside. It looked so strange to have that monster car in this historic little town, and then, to discover that they were waiting for *us*. One of the men jumped out of the car, and said he wanted Jonathan and me to attend a party; that everyone was waiting for us, and they'd drive us there. Jonathan was reluctant; after all, it was around 11:30 p.m., but I, being a party girl at heart, liked the idea and cajoled and convinced him. Once we got inside the limo, which was equipped with a huge bar, we met a few more men, and they gave us drinks. After we were driving and drinking for a while, I began thinking, "They could be kidnapping us," and "Maybe they gave us a knock-out drink." (I'd been in too many melodramas!) When I couldn't figure out *why* they would want to abduct us, I relaxed, and at that point, we arrived at the house and the party. It seems that word got around that *DS* stars were at the mansion, and since everyone who was anyone (in Milledgeville) was at the party, the party's hosts wanted us there, too. We stayed at the party for about an hour and then got them to drive us home since David had arranged early morning interviews for us with the local newspaper.

There were many morning newspaper and radio interviews. David always picked me up at the mansion and we drove to them together. He was the host on one of the radio shows and we did a really good interview one morning. Because he knew me quite well by then, he asked lots of out-of-the-ordinary questions about *Dark Shadows*, Broadway shows I had been featured in, and of course, his present production of *The Lion in Winter*.

We continued working on the play for a few more weeks and then opened. The only downside was that we played for such a short period. But that's the nature of college productions. Everyone works very hard, often coming up with a wonderful production and then the show opens and closes within a week. My buddy from *Carousel*, Nancy Eaton, drove over from Charleston with her friend (who soon became my friend, too), an artist named Linda Vinson, and they saw our Saturday night performance. We had one last performance on Sunday afternoon and a closing party at the Moore home. Everyone was sad to see the play end, but had a wonderful time partying and saying good-bye. The next morning I drove off with my friends and made my first of many trips to Charleston.

I returned to Georgia College several times after that, but without Jonathan. David invited me back to play Madame X in August Strindberg's *The Stronger*. That was a powerful play to work on—a one-act play between two women, with one character doing all the talking while the other one stays mute. It's really a dramatic monologue. You can imagine which role I chose to play (the one with all the lines, natch). The play takes place on Christmas Eve as Madame X (my character) confronts Mademoiselle Y, her husband's former mistress. Although Y has nothing to say, all of her reactions feed my character, and Jessica Raymer, the young actress who played the part, gave me everything I needed. The question at the end is "Who is the stronger?" We left the audience guessing. We had a week's break during my time there, when the kids traveled to Savannah for the Southeastern Theatre Conference (SETC) auditions. David took me along and I got a chance to enjoy another great southern city.

Living at the mansion alone was a different experience than with Jonathan. There was a small elevator that I avoided at night, because I was afraid that if *it* got stuck, *I* would be stuck for the night because no one else was in the house. (Remember that this was in the days before cell phones.) The stairs were creaky, but there was dead silence, too, and then sudden sounds I'd never heard before. My imagination ran wild and I envisioned ghosts and locked my doors and sang out loud so I'd scare the ghosts away. Shades of *Dark Shadows!* Twice, the Fire Department had to come in because I burned some toast and it set off an alarm. One night, when I arrived home, I forgot to turn off the security alarm, and I had just climbed the three flights to my suite, when I heard voices and footsteps on the stairs behind me. I froze for a moment until they identified themselves as college security, checking to make sure no one had broken into the mansion. After that, I relaxed because I knew I was fully protected.

I went back once more to do the *Festival of Original One-Act Plays*. The students presented plays they had directed and some that they had written. I was the hostess throughout with a running commentary on the writer/students. It was great to be back at the mansion and to work with David and many of the same students, and since the work wasn't as challenging, we had time for a lot more fun and games.

David eventually decided to return to the professional theatre world and moved to New York. I was delighted that he lived in my city, but was sorry not to be able to appear on the Georgia College stage with him again and live in luxury at the mansion. The upside is that I see David on a regular basis and we always have a great time together. And I'm delighted to have worked with Jonathan Frid again, in such a good play, in what he often calls his "directorial debut." It was a great experience for me—being directed by Jonathan, and experiencing his enormous skill in theatre craft. I should have known he'd be a good director, since he writes, produces, acts, *and* directs all his one-man shows. I hope one day to get another opportunity to work with him.

Blowing Rock

What a pleasure it was to be up in the mountains during the hot sweltering summer of 1993. I spent the month of July in North Carolina, and it was 99 degrees and more every day down in town, but our little theatre was on top of the cool mountain. Don't be mislead, it wasn't a wild uninhabited mountain; Blowing Rock has charming Bed-and-Breakfasts, a storybook village with great antique shops and attractive restaurants, and is actually a winter ski resort, but it's also a great place to escape from it all in the summer. In fact, many affluent Southerners build second homes in the mountains for their long summer vacations, and they often use them during the skiing season. But the true-blue skiers, who are only interested in the snow, rent out their homes in the summertime. The end result is that we actors got to stay in great places. In some theatre locations around the country, housing accommodations can be sub-standard, but that kind of housing doesn't exist in Blowing Rock. My guess is that it cost the producers more money for our housing than they paid us in salary. We worked under what actors call a *Spit Contract*, which is more commonly called an S.P.T., and stands for *Small Professional Theatre* contract. We nicknamed it *Spit* because that's just about what we got paid. On the other hand, we didn't lose money doing it, and best of all, especially with the first play I did there, it was like a paid vacation.

But I'm jumping ahead—there was an audition first, which was arranged by agent Louis Chambers, who told me that the producing director of the Blowing Rock Stage Company, Mark Wilson, wanted actors to audition with a monologue of their choice. I'm much more comfortable preparing a scene from the play I'm reading for, rather than choosing a monologue from a different play, and so I was reluctant to go. But Louis said that Mark was a great *Dark Shadows* fan, and I should just go to the audition and meet him and he would probably let me have my own way and give me the script to read. So I went over to the Actors' Equity Building on West 46th Street at my appointed hour and met with him. After a nice long chat, he gave me a scene from the play to read cold (without preparation). The reason that he hadn't given the play to agents was that it was a new, as-yet unpublished play, and he didn't want it to be all over town before it was in print. The play was *Nuptials*, a comedy about the chaos and confusion that erupts as everyone in town interferes with a bride and groom in their wedding preparations. North Carolina playwright Judy Simpson Cook wrote it. I played the wedding planner, Jeannette Stovall, the most interfering of the whole bunch.

Mark had come to the city to cast the entire summer's program, so when he picked me for the part, it was another six weeks before I went down/up there, ("down" because it's North Carolina and south of New York, and "up" 'cause it's the mountains). On July 11, I flew out of LaGuardia Airport with seven other actors heading to Greensboro, North Carolina, for the start of a good theatre experience. We were picked up in Greensboro by Mark and the managing director, Jerry Burns, and driven to the theatre, stopping for a delicious dinner along the way. By the time we arrived at our houses, it felt like we'd known each other for years. I shared a house with two of the actresses from the show, Karin Wolfe (Barbara, mother of the bride) and Mary Lucy Bibins (Mae-Ella, the housekeeper). It was a log house (not a cabin, it was three stories high), with a deck that overlooked a wooded area. We all loved the house, remarked that we felt like we were on vacation, and then realized it was midnight and we'd better get to bed because we had a 10 a.m. rehearsal call. We knew that we were in for a good couple of weeks, so we all went to sleep content.

I got up early the next day to walk the country roads and get a lay of the land. It's very hilly there so it was a good workout. I then met Karin and we had a chance to walk around Blowing Rock before rehearsals, and we fell in love with the town. There were flowers everywhere, with hanging plants on each lamppost, and charming alleys with unique shops and restaurants. We had a running dialogue about what kind of shop we could open there, ready to move at a moment's notice. Reality would then set in, and I knew I loved New York so much that I could never live in a small town on a regular basis, but it's fun to dream about the possibilities.

Our rehearsals were in a school next door to the theatre, and we worked from 10 a.m. to 7:30 p.m., with an hour-and-a-half lunch break. Karin and I ate fast and ran around the town to see what else was there. We discovered a small lake with a path around it, which turned out to be a good place for my race-walking. We also found the starting point of a hiking trail, and we promised each other that on our first day off, we would take the hike. Then we rushed back to school and our rehearsals.

Nuptials is a light, fluffy play and perfect for the venue. Jeannette is a supporting role, and I was in scenes scattered throughout the play. Chuck Rounds was the play's director, and he considerately divided the rehearsals up, so that I only had to be there for a certain amount of hours. I'd then go back to my place, get into my hiking clothes, and hike *down* the mountain. That took a while to get used to, since you nearly always go *up* the mountain first, and then come down. But we were at an elevation of 4,000 feet so there was nowhere to go but down. You really had to pace yourself, keeping in mind that you had to ascend later, because "what goes down, must come up," (especially in Blowing Rock, as you'll soon learn). There were well-mapped trails, and it wasn't hard going, but it was tiring after a few hours. Other times, I rode the courtesy bus to a big park and race-walked there for an hour, or just walked on the back roads. I even got lost a few times but I eventually found my way back. Drivers were always so polite, offering to pick me up and give me a lift home. No one ever believed I really wanted to walk—no one walks in the country; that's a big city activity. But as much as I enjoyed playing, I was there to do the work, and it turned out to be equally delightful. The one critic in Blowing Rock felt the same way:

"*Nuptials* brings to the Blowing Rock stage not only one of the strongest casts in the eight-year history of the Stage Company but also one of its more clever scripts. Marie Wallace as the snotty wedding director is also terrific. 'I don't like that character,' I heard someone say during the intermission, 'but the woman playing her is doing a super job.'"—Becky Steele, *The Blowing Rocket*

There is actually a spot called Blowing Rock, and it's a tourist attraction, so of course I went there. I love being a tourist; I often even act like one in New York. I'm constantly discovering new places there; streets I've never walked, pocket parks I don't know about, shops, a new gallery, an interesting restaurant, and all sorts of exciting things. I think everyone should treat their hometown that way—it opens you to new adventures, and that's always exciting. Consequently, when friends come to visit me, wherever I am, where do I take them first? To the biggest attraction in town. So when my friends, Nancy Eaton (from *Carousel*) and Linda Vinson (artist from Charleston) came to see the play, naturally I became the tour guide and showed off the big attraction. It's an immense cliff 4,000 feet above sea level, overhanging Johns River Gorge 3,000 feet below. The winds sweep against the rocky walls of the gorge and send back objects that have been thrown over the void. And the legend is that a Cherokee brave leaped from The Rock into the wilderness below while his grief-stricken girlfriend watched. She prayed daily to the Great Spirit to return her lover and one evening, a gust of wind blew him back into her arms. There's a Ripley's "Believe-It-Or-Not" cartoon that states, "It's the only place in the world where snow falls upside down." Everyone threw something down but only the lightest objects returned—the bottom of that gorge must be very well littered at this point.

When Mark Wilson, the show's producer/director, came to New York the following winter, I kept in mind what a great fan of *Dark Shadows* he is. I arranged a meeting with Jonathan Frid and Louis Edmonds to meet Mark (my friend David Moore, who already knew Mark, was there too). We spent a delightful afternoon with Mark in Jonathan's apartment, even talking about the possibility of doing a show with Louis, Jonathan and me, some time in the future. At one point, Louis, in his grand manner, said to Mark, "Tell me, dear boy, what is the *name* of your theatre?" Mark replied, "Blowing Rock." And Louis said, dragging out the words in his most melodious, mellifluous tones, "Blowing Rock. What an unfortunate name!" Mark almost fell off his seat, but we all laughed, and so did Mark, eventually. Louis had a way of delivering a line that could be devastating, but it was always meant to be funny.

None of the plays in their next two seasons had parts that I was remotely right for. And in '96, I looked over the list of plays they would be doing and again, nothing seemed to suit me. But then I got a call from Mark, asking me about the classic comedy *Arsenic and Old Lace*. At first, I thought that the play wasn't for me, since there were only two good female parts and they were real character parts; old biddies/grandma types. But I studied the play and realized how good it is, and what a challenge it would be to play either one of the women. No one would cast me for those parts on TV or in New York, so why not take this opportunity, especially since I loved the theatre and town so much. That's one of the reasons I always encourage young (and old) actors to work in regional or summer theatre. It's an invaluable training ground. There's often a chance to play a variety of roles, some that an actor might not be physically right for, but would be a challenge for him. On Broadway, and especially on TV, producers seldom take chances, and they usually look for someone who is "right on the nose." Classes and workshops are invaluable too, but the good thing here is that the theatre pays the actor, not the other way around.

Mark and I talked and he decided that I should play Martha Brewster. The part of her sister, Abby, would be played by Mary Lucy Bivins. She had played the maid in *Nuptials*, and I knew we'd have a good time working together. Mark put together another brilliant cast, which included Leonard Drum, Allen Lewis Rickman, A. W. Schmitz, Michele Ammon, L. J. Ganser, J. C. Hoyt, and Chip Stelz. This time it wasn't such a vacation, since Mary Lucy and I were both on stage a great deal of the time, but I managed to do an hour's walk every morning before rehearsals and that got me in shape for the day. We had a great deal of fun rehearsing this wild play and once again, the critic in Blowing Rock loved it as much as we did:

"Director Chuck Rounds and his incredibly talented cast give subtle nuances to the characters that make their production a true delight. The performers make the characters their own with those detailed touches that make this production so much fun.... The Brewster sisters, played by Mary Lucy Bivins and Marie Wallace, are just perfect. They have a terrific rapport and they are just as delightfully charming as they can be. Bivins and Wallace are true stars on the stage."—Becky Steele, *The Blowing Rocket*

Once the play opened, I had the whole day free for fun and games, except on matinee days, so I once more got into my hiking mode. My brother Billy and sister Dolly (the twins) drove down during the run and spent a few days with me, and Nancy Eaton drove over from Charleston. We try to see each other's work as much as we can, and I have often flown down to Charleston to see her perform in the Spoleto Festival. I love that town, and of course I love my dear friends who live there.

The two experiences at Blowing Rock Stage didn't last for long periods, but the memories are very strong. I'm pleased to have had the opportunity to be there with Mark Wilson and his crew, both for the work and the downtime.

Photography: A New Beginning

As the wise songwriter and philosopher John Lennon said, "Life is what happens while you're busy making other plans." I've certainly found that to be true in my own journey. We think we've made very clear-cut choices, when in reality, it's chance that often directs our lives. Missing a plane, turning one corner rather than the other, going to a party instead of the movies, talking to one person instead of another, being late or early for an appointment.... Each of these actions can introduce another set of circumstances into our lives, and *va-va-voom!*, we're off in a new direction, sometimes headed for a new beginning with a surprise outcome that's better than anything we might have dreamed of.

Photography was like that for me. For many years, I thought of it as a hobby, a diversion, done for the fun and love of it. You'll recall that I got my first Konica 35mm camera as a birthday present during the run of *Sly Fox*. When I returned from the tour, I wanted to learn all I could about photography, so I got my then-boyfriend, Bob, to set up his dark room. He hadn't used it since his college days and it had been disassembled and tucked away in a storage closet. He was such a good photographer, though a lawyer by profession, and I thought that he could give me a few pointers on technique. Wrong!!! He wasn't a good teacher, since he had no patience, so I turned to books and to just doing it. I'd go running around Central Park with my Konica around my neck and some black-and-white film in my pocket and photograph animals, kids, and old folks. In addition to the very sharp 50mm lens that I received with the camera, I bought a 200mm telephoto lens so I could shoot from a distance with my subjects unaware of my presence (which came in especially handy in Central Park). I'd then run back and develop the film and print a contact sheet. Bob did teach me some of the fundamentals, and technique books taught me the rest.

I had the ABCs down, but I needed some expert help, so I signed up for a Saturday class in darkroom technique at Stuyvesant High School. I went there every Saturday morning while Bob went to his country club to play golf. Since I love sports, I could have gone with Bob, but I found being in the darkroom much more exciting than riding a golf cart and swinging a club. The photography class was elementary and the school's darkroom was full of dust (which can be disastrous for your negatives), but it didn't matter. The teacher was passionate about his subject, and he created an excitement that rubbed off on all of his students.

The first thing I learned was how to remove exposed film from its cartridge and load it onto a spiral in a changing bag. Up to that point, I had been going into a completely blacked-out closet, struggling with the film, sweating profusely, getting very nervous, and usually calling in Bob to finish the job. The changing bag changed all that for me. It probably had something to do with being in a completely lit room, with only my hands in the dark inside the bag. It was a simpler task that way. After that, the loaded spiral is placed into the developing tank, and the developer solution is poured in. I then learned the importance of agitating the tank for ten seconds during each minute of recommended development time, and the value of rapping the tank on the table after each shakeup. That ensured the even flow of the solution and the removal of air bubbles—two techniques that help to ensure a much better negative. That may be more than you want to know about developing a negative, but I was getting serious and being very precise. I was enjoying every moment of it, and was thrilled to be learning this type of detail, and to be exposed to the techniques of a serious photographer.

We also printed enlargements in class, and learned the darkroom method of dodging (using a tool to suppress light from an area of print that's too dark), and burning-in (the opposite of dodging, to give more exposure to light areas). I was being drawn into photography, and during and after the course, I shot loads of black-and-white film and used the home-darkroom every chance I could get. I felt like a kid starting at the kindergarten level and earnestly working my way up. I never imagined that my efforts in the darkroom could teach me so much about how to shoot a photograph. By looking at the results floating in my sink, I could analyze and evaluate my successes and failures, and on my next outing, I had a chance to try it in a different way.

I also had studied with a photographer when I was living in California, to develop my shooting skills, and soon signed up for a course at International Center for Photography (ICP) in New York. I only went there for three weeks because by the fourth week, I had gotten an acting job and was on my way out of town. After all, I was still, first and foremost, an actress. Yet as time went by, I yearned to know everything about photography, so I took more photography classes and workshops, and joined a camera club. But it still hadn't occurred to me that I might be training myself for a new profession. I had been an actress all my adult life and I didn't think anything would ever replace that. But I was accepting more and more photography assignments, mostly headshots for actors, and programs and pamphlets for the Periwinkle National Theatre. (I knew the founder and executive director, Sunna Rasch, from my early acting days.) I still thought of the photography assignments as interim jobs, something to occupy my time while I was "between-engagements." However, slowly but surely, I had more and more photography jobs, with less and less time for show biz. Even so, if someone asked me, "What do you do?" I'd say, "I'm an actress." Then without consciously changing it, my answer became "Actress and photographer." Then it became "Photographer/actress," which eventually turned into "Photographer."

The first time I ever exhibited a photograph, I was still an amateur, and I won the first place award (the details of the contest are in my "East Meets West" chapter). Receiving that award was a little like getting my first theatrical job. I was especially proud of that photo because I had not only taken it with my Konica camera, 200mm lens, but I also had developed the film, and printed the 8x10. I had shot it in my favorite New York City locale, Central Park, and I titled it *Reverie*. It's of an old man, leaning his face and hand against a rock, and the texture of his skin and the rock are the same. He seems to be staring off into his own world. In fact, he was watching a clown entertain a group of kids. Whenever I see street entertainment, I almost never take a photo of the one performing (except when I'm the hired photographer for the event). I'm usually fascinated by the viewers' reactions to the performer because that's where you find the interesting picture. That award was most gratifying, and since then, I've received a few others that I'm proud of, from contests at the Arts Interaction Gallery:

Honorable Mention—Black & White Division—*Mary*

First Place—Color Collage—*World Trade Center #1*

Honorable Mention—Group *of Six Photos*

First Place—Color Division—*L .A. Freeway*

Second Place—Black & White Division—*Private Moment*

Ida Glueckselig Memorial Award—Color Division—*Presbyterian Rose*

I've had several photography exhibits and in June 1995, my first solo show was handled by the Arts Interaction Gallery, and shown at Coogan's Restaurant in New York. Preparing for a show is labor-intensive, but I've always enjoyed the process of going through my work, making choices, and having them printed. I stopped doing the printing myself because it got too time-consuming. I began by doing the matting and framing of the photos, but when I found myself still working at two in the morning, I decided to have the rest done by a professional framer. It was an eclectic mixture of my work. I presented twenty-five of my photographs and sold twelve (*Presbyterian Rose* and *L. A. Freeway* were the most popular and I had to make up extra prints to fill the orders.) I liked that a lot! Later I had my Central Park Exhibit, which is one of my favorites and I feature it on my

Web site (www.mariewallace.com). It was held at the West Side Y in Manhattan. My childhood and my dear mother were the inspiration for those photos. Mom always made sure her children got away to the country and camp every summer. And when we couldn't trek to the real country, we just took a quick walk of seven blocks up to Fifth Avenue and *Central Park*. The photography exhibit is a tribute to the park and I accompanied it with this essay:

> I grew up in New York, and some of my fondest memories take place in Central Park. It was our "backyard" and we used it for everything. What magic! At the carousel—reaching for the golden ring…and at Pilgrim Hill—sleigh riding in the winter, and simply rolling down the grassy hill in summer…at the 72nd Street Mall—walking up the Promenade from 60th Street on Sundays to hear the Goldman Band concerts, and square-dancing and jitterbugging on Tuesday and Thursday nights. Then there were the football/soccer/baseball fields where we cheered on our brothers and boyfriends, and the 63rd Street "diamonds" where I played first base on the Broadway Show League's softball teams.
>
> I also have fond memories of…rowing at the "rowboat lake" with my girlfriends, flirting with the boys on their boats…playing tennis at the 92nd Street courts…jogging around the reservoir before it was a fashionable activity…outdoor dining at Tavern on the Green, a tourist spot to some, but one of my favorite places in the spring. And what a pleasure it was back in the late sixties and seventies to go to Bethesda Fountain and sit in the outdoor restaurant at the foot of the stairs, people-watching.
>
> One of the biggest thrills in the park is the Philharmonic concerts and fireworks, which friends and I have relished since they began—first at Sheep Meadow and now at the Great Lawn. The Shakespeare Gardens, the Zoo, the Rambles; the list goes on and on, and now that I live directly across from the park, I continue to get great joy from it every day.
>
> Things have changed in New York since I was a kid growing up in Yorkville—many for the better, a few for the worse—but the park gets better and better each year.
>
> If asked why I live in New York, my first response would be, "because of Central Park."

I continued to exhibit, often just one or two photos in large exhibits with many other photographers, and then I had a two-woman show with my friend, writer and photographer Joan Penn. That was an exhibit on Ireland, and it was back at Coogan's once again. We had each gone separately to Ireland the year before, and we had many photos we loved and wanted to display. Joan and I were both grateful to Coogan's owners, Peter Walsh and David Hunt, for opening their restaurant for our exhibit and hosting a great opening-night party.

These days, my professional work in the photography field is as a Special Events Photographer, and every day brings a new and different event, some more intriguing than others. I shoot galas, ribbon-cutting and groundbreaking ceremonies, opening nights, celebrity hospital visits, charity affairs and street fairs—everything but weddings and bar mitzvahs. (They're too high-pressure to be much fun.)

I have a number of clients in the city, although New York Presbyterian Hospital keeps me so busy, I hardly have time for anyone else. Joan Penn introduced me to the Public Relations Department there over ten years ago. It started out as a few jobs here and there and grew into full-time work. I get assignments from at least ten different departments at the hospital, and my photographs appear in their newsletters, brochures, posters, and annual reports. I've also created a number of permanent exhibits there, and it's fun to walk through the various departments and see my enlarged and framed photographs.

One of the most satisfying parts of photography is going out on my own and exploring with my camera. As happens in a good acting scene, my entire being is immersed into what I'm doing. There's a feeling of connection with the earth that's especially strong in the countryside, in the early morning, with diffused sunlight. It's as though I'm discovering every leaf, branch, flower, and tree; it can be magical. I love flower photography and experimenting with apertures, often using the widest aperture and focusing in on one part of the flower. Shooting leaves is fun, looking for shapes, textures, patterns, again making them abstracts by removing extraneous detail and getting in very close. An overcast day provides great opportunities too, with light that brings out the intensity in trees and grass. Somehow I see so much more when my camera is with me.

Someone once said to me that it seemed to him that photography is such a lonely pursuit. And that surprised me, because I've always felt that when I'm with my camera, I'm never alone. In fact, I much prefer to go out shooting by myself than with a companion or a group. When I went out on photography excursions with the Park West Camera Club—the best club in the country—I still preferred to wander off by myself. Nonetheless, I continually went back to our leader, Chuck Pine, for his advice and guidance. I learned so much from him; most especially every spring when he conducted his "Expanding Visions" classes, with assignments that opened my mind to so many photographic possibilities. Each week brought a new theme: reflections, zoom effect, panning with slow shutter speeds, soft focus, and best of all, "breaking the rules."

Even just this little bit of advice, "You're never in the right spot," keeps me moving to the right, the left, lower, higher, and helps create much more attention-grabbing pictures. It's a constant learning experience. When I saw that a commonplace object could be given new significance just by the shooting angle, I was amazed—the ordinary turned into a work of art! We often start to shoot from one vantage point and get stuck there, not budging from the spot until we're finished. Sometimes that can be just perfect, but other times there's a more interesting angle just a foot away. The discoveries go on and on; it's absorbing and can keep me busy for hours. How lucky I am, that I went down a path by chance and found something so satisfying.

Over this past decade, I have continued to do theatre and television, but you can see how my interests have slowly turned in another direction: to my photography, traveling with good friends, and simply enjoying life to its fullest. I love the acting profession, and now, I have that same love for my photography, knowing it isn't a job "between engagements," but a distinctive and satisfying career. And I'm still open to all the possibilities that are out there, of making an unplanned turn on a road, and ending up in yet another profession, or perhaps taking an old familiar path, which would lead me to a place where once more, when asked my profession, I would happily answer, "Actress!"

Jonathan, Marie, the Lion, and Me: A Note from David Moore

"And of course, you know Marie from the show, don't you David?" Jonathan Frid asked in his inimitable booming baritone.

I smiled and nodded at our host for brunch, and was delighted to be sitting next to this beautiful, vivacious woman. As luck would have it, between the restaurant's waterfall and mariachi band, we could only hear the people right next to us. "What shows are you doing at your theatre next year?" Marie asked, and when I told her we were to open our season with one of my favorite musicals, *Gypsy*, she said, "That was my first Broadway show." I was immediately hooked.

This was during the 1992 *Dark Shadows* Festival in Los Angles. At the time, I had put my acting/directing career on hold and was the director of theatre at Georgia College in my hometown of Milledgeville. Jonathan had visited our campus the previous year with his one-man show. He had enjoyed his visit, so I had been trying to coax him into appearing in one of our productions as a guest artist. Although he wasn't interested in acting at that time, he did say he'd always wanted to direct. I thought he'd be the perfect director for *The Lion in Winter*, and a deal was struck.

Some months after the Festival, as Jonathan and I discussed the upcoming production, we agreed that a professional guest artist rather than a college student really should play the pivotal role of Eleanor, and he suggested Marie. A few phone conversations with Marie (and Actors' Equity) later, it was a done deal.

During the Christmas break before we began *Lion* rehearsals in January, I made one of my regular theatre trips to New York. When Marie found out I was going to be in town, she hosted a wonderful dinner party. Jonathan was there, and what a fantastic evening it was, hearing his and Marie's fascinating stories about all the great theatre they'd done, working with so many legends in the business.

Marie came to Georgia in early January. She and Jonathan stayed in the Old Governor's Mansion on our campus. (Milledgeville had been the state capitol during the Civil War but was not destroyed by Sherman on his March to the Sea. Eventually, the mansion was turned over to the college and now housed a museum downstairs, and the college president's office and a few guest quarters upstairs.) Jonathan and Marie were gracious guests, and the mansion's staff treated them like royalty.

After the students auditioned for the play, Jonathan felt that no one was quite right for the role of Eleanor's oldest son, Richard.... No one except me, that is. Although I was looking forward to having one rehearsal period in our season off (we had produced six shows in nine months), I jumped at the chance to work with such accomplished artists.

In spite of how challenging a play *Lion* is, we had great fun in and out of rehearsal. During one of our long technical rehearsals, which can be tedious, we all got a bad case of hysterics when Jonathan referred to his assistant director Johnettta as Josette, which was the name of his character's long-time love on *Dark Shadows*.

Since the students were in class during the day, we only rehearsed at night, leaving lots of free time for our guest artists. Jonathan and Marie immediately became fixtures on the civic lunch club circuit in our small town, making appearances to promote the show. Each of them appeared on a live morning radio talk show I hosted, as well as television talk shows in Macon and Atlanta. We also got great newspaper coverage, with lots of articles, interviews, and photos.

The nature of my job was pretty time-consuming. I administered the theatre program and taught classes during the day, and most nights and weekends were spent in rehearsal. Consequently, I kept a pretty low social profile; my schedule precluded me from attending many parties. However, once word of Jonathan and Marie's residency spread, I started getting *lots* of party invitations...some from people I hardly knew—and in some cases, didn't know at all. Each was the same: After a gracious invitation, when I mentioned that I was hosting some guest artists, I'd be told, "Oh well, feel free to bring them along—*please!*" Our social calendar got so busy we appointed Marie "social chairman" to coordinate our bookings and appearances.

Marie stays in excellent shape through regular exercise. I, on the other hand, have always been a bit of a couch potato. When Marie discovered that there was a beautiful walking trail in a park on the opposite side of town from campus, she asked if I'd take her there after classes. And of course, she said, since I was going to be there with her, why not join her in some fitness walking? I did, and we had great fun, running our lines and having long talks as we race-walked. We became very close friends during those walks.

Marie was wonderful with my students. They learned so much from her, even during casual conversations. Once, a student who had trouble projecting his voice admitted to her that he got nervous before going onstage. "I do, too," Marie said, "but I just take a deep breath, go out there and be as loud as I can be. The louder I am, the less nervous I am." I doubt Marie was nervous, but her quick thinking solved two problems at once: The student relaxed and he spoke up. (Incidentally, all those students have done well, acting in various theatres all over the country; one has spent a few years in the Broadway tour of *Les Misérables*, another had a national Visa commercial, and still another is a dentist with a thriving practice outside Atlanta.)

It seemed that almost as soon as we began rehearsals, the show was coming to a close. We had a wonderful cast party, and Marie, never one to let grass grow under her feet, left straight from the party to a getaway with friends in Charleston before heading back to New York.

I hired Marie again to host our annual One Act Play Festival for the next two years, once a season until I left Georgia and headed to New York to return to acting and directing full-time. We've had many wonderful times together since then; I've even accompanied her to various *Dark Shadows* events. That is always great fun. She's beloved by the show's fans (they know that the Marie they meet at the *DS* Fests is the real Marie: charming, witty, kind, intelligent, and practical). At the *DS* Fests, when she refers to me by name, some fans assume that, since I'm about the right age and coloring, I must be David Henesy, one of her co-stars from the show.

Although Marie and I haven't done any more shows together (yet!), we have enjoyed many great meals, movies, plays, and yes, even some more exercise.

Career Highlights

BROADWAY

Gypsy	Chorus	with Ethel Merman
The Beauty Part	Roxana DeVilbiss	with Bert Lahr
The Right Honourable Gentle-man	Helen Garland	with Coral Browne
Nobody Loves an Albatross	Linda	with Robert Preston
		Gene Saks, Director
Sweet Charity	Ursula	with Gwen Verdon
		Bob Fosse, Director
The Women	Crystal Allen	Mort DaCosta, Director
Mert & Phil	The Beauty Lady	with Estelle Parsons
		Joseph Papp, Director

TELEVISION

Dark Shadows	Eve
Dark Shadows	Jenny Collins (Crazy Jenny)
Dark Shadows	Megan Todd
Somerset	India Delaney
Guiding Light	Johnsie LaFite
One Life to Live	Molly O'Day
Fantasy Island	Mrs. Vinton, Co-star role
Fame	Mrs. Murphy, Co-star role

REGIONAL THEATRE

Who's Afraid of Virginia Woolf?	Martha	Capital Repertory
The Night of the Iguana	Maxine Faulk	Meadow Brook Theatre
Born Yesterday	Billie Dawn	Meadow Brook Theatre
The Lion in Winter	Eleanor of Aquitaine	Georgia College Theatre
The Stronger	Madame X	Georgia College Theatre
Listen to the Lions	Fuzzy Delgato	Aspen Playwrights Conference
Arsenic and Old Lace	Martha Brewster	Blowing Rock Stage
Nuptials	Jeannette Stovall	Blowing Rock Stage
Mummer's End	Peaches O'Rourke	Folger Theatre
Angel Street	Nancy	The Theatre in Westchester

NATIONAL TOUR

Carousel	Mrs. Mullin	with Robert Goulet
		James Hammerstein, Director
Sly Fox	Miss Fancy	with Jackie Gleason
		Arthur Penn, Director

DINNER THEATRE

Forty Carats	Ann Stanley	Country Dinner Playhouse
Alone Together	Helene	Firehouse Theatre
Goodbye Charlie	Rusty	Club Bene with Fannie Flagg

SUMMER THEATRE

The Night of the Iguana	Maxine Faulk	Hampton Playhouse
The Ladies Bump	Rose LaMarr	
Enter Laughing	Angela	

Burlesque	Bonny
Strip for Action	Janet
Bachelor's Honeymoon	Eadie
The Star-Spangled Girl	Sophie Rauschmeyer
The Only Game in Town	Fran
I Ought to Be in Pictures	Steffy

OFF-BROADWAY

Sophocles' *Electra* & *Harlequinade* (double bill)	Greek chorus Joyce Langland	Rita Allen Theatre
The Lark	Queen Yolanda	York Theatre Company
In the Boom Boom Room	Helen	South Street Theatre
Barflys, Part I	Connie Mae	Courtyard Theatre

And of course, the Park Avenue Players

About the Author

Marie Wallace found herself drawn to the footlights at an early age. She appeared in her first professional production, Off-Broadway, as a teenager. She also modeled, both on the runway and in print.

In 1959, Marie landed her first Broadway show: as one of the showgirls in the original production of *Gypsy*, starring Ethel Merman. Her list of Broadway credits grew to include *The Beauty Part* (1962-63); *Nobody Loves an Albatross* (1963-64), with Robert Preston; *The Right Honourable Gentleman* (1965-66) with Coral Browne and Frances Sternhagen; *Sweet Charity* (1966-67) starring Gwen Verdon and Ruth Buzzi, and directed by Bob Fosse; *Mert & Phil* with Estelle Parsons and Beverlee McKinsey, and directed by Joe Papp; and *The Women* (1973) with Myrna Loy and Kim Hunter. She also toured the U.S. with Jackie Gleason in *Sly Fox* and with Robert Goulet in *Carousel*.

On TV, Marie has guest-starred in such classics as *Car 54 Where Are You?*, *The Phil Silvers Show*, *Fame*, and *Fantasy Island*, as well as many commercials.

Marie played three roles on the Gothic soap opera *Dark Shadows*, beginning in 1968: evil Eve, Crazy Jenny Collins, and vicious vampire Megan Todd. Megan became a vampire, and the day the character met her demise, Marie got a call from her agent with another job. "I said, 'I've just been staked,' I'd better take it!," she recalled years later. Marie then moved to NBC and originated the character India Delaney on the 1970 *Another World* spin-off *Somerset*. Other soap opera roles have included Johnsie Lafite on *Guiding Light*, and Molly O'Day on *One Life To Live*.

She's been a fan favorite at the annual *Dark Shadows* Festivals, often performing dramatic one-woman shows and readings. In the winter of 1993, Marie worked with *DS* star Jonathan Frid as he made his directing debut with a stage production of *The Lion in Winter*, at the Georgia College Theatre in Milledgeville, Georgia. Heading up a cast of students, Marie played Eleanor of Aquitaine.

For more information, visit Marie's official site, www.mariewallace.com, part of DarkShadowsOnline.com.

—Craig Hamrick
Author, *Barnabas & Co: The Cast of the Cult Classic Dark Shadows*
New York City
May 2005

978-0-595-35877-9
0-595-35877-2

Printed in the United States
53289LVS00003B/355-417

9 780595 358779